ILLUSTRATED ENCYC

CIGARS
OF THE WORLD

ILLUSTRATED ENCYCLOPEDIA

CIGARS
OF THE WORLD

JULIAN HOLLAND
CONSULTANT: NEIL MILLINGTON

SELECT
EDITIONS

Select Editions imprint specially produced for Selectabook Ltd

© Anness Publishing Limited 1999

Produced by Anness Publishing Limited
Hermes House, 88-89 Blackfriars Road, London SE1 8HA

ISBN 1-84081-243-5

A CIP catalogue record for this book is available from the British Library

Publisher: Joanna Lorenz
Senior Editor: Lindsay Porter
Editorial Assistant: Kathrin Henkel
Project Editor: Felicity Forster
UK Research: InfoSearch
US Research: Shannon Ryan, Amy Wilensky
Designer: Nigel Partridge
Cover Design: Balley Design Associates
Photographers: Walt Chrynwski, John Freeman, Dave Jordan

Also published as *The New Guide to Cigars* and, as part of a larger compendium,
The Ultimate Cigar Encyclopedia

Printed and bound in Hong Kong
1 3 5 7 9 10 8 6 4 2

ACKNOWLEDGEMENTS
The Publishers would like to thank the following for their assistance in producing this book:
Neil Millington; Alfred Dunhill Ltd; Desmond Sautter of Sautter's of Mayfair; Tim Cox of J.J. Fox's;
Harrods Cigar Room; The London Cigar Importing Co. Ltd; N.R. Silverstone Ltd; Premium Cigar Ltd;
Rothmans International; Swisher International Ltd; Valdrych Cigars.

CONTENTS

INTRODUCTION

Cigar smoking is currently enjoying a renaissance. The demand for premium handmade cigars often exceeds supply, and cigar aficionados are prepared to pay large amounts of money to luxuriate in their aroma and taste. Currently, the largest proportion of handmade cigars is only available in the United States – by far the largest consumer, thanks partly to the stars of cinema and TV, who have widely publicized their enjoyment of the habit. Out of a total of over 1,000 brands, about 90 % can be bought in the United States, while only 15 % can be purchased in the UK. However, this small percentage does include the availability of most Havana cigars, due to the continuing US embargo on Cuban goods.

Cigars are smoked slowly, for relaxation and enjoyment, or for their flavour and aroma during contemplative moments. Serious cigar smokers have strong preferences for particular brands and loyalty to the shops that supply them. In the early days of World War II, Winston Churchill received a message from the manager of Dunhill, whose shop had just been bombed: "Your cigars are safe, Sir". It is rumoured that prior to the US trade embargo on Cuba, President John F. Kennedy ordered stocks of his favourite Havanas.

Both of these anecdotes reveal the importance of the cigar to the connoisseur: they are appreciated, discussed and studied in much the same way as a vintage wine or fine whisky. A premium cigar has qualities that depend upon

ABOVE AND LEFT: A cigar cutter and amber cheroot holder. Early smoking accessories are now highly collectable.

BELOW: Bundles of premium cigars, grouped according to colour.

ABOVE: Elaborately painted cases for "segars", as they were called in the 19th century.

where the tobacco was grown, how it was fermented, the blend of the leaves and the skill of the makers – each stage in the process is handled by an expert in that particular skill, whether stripping the leaves or rolling the tobacco.

Because of the time and expertise required to create high-quality cigars, they are not cheap – this does not mean that only the very wealthy smoke cigars, however. Recent years have seen a renaissance in cigar smoking and appreciation, with specialist shops, clubs and restaurants devoted to the pleasures of smoking cigars. For the newcomer to this fascinating world, the wide variety of cigar types may seem bewildering. This book aims to demystify the subject and to enhance the enjoyment and pleasure of anyone who appreciates a cigar.

RIGHT: A metal case for carrying a single cigar, from the late 19th century.

CUBA

❦

The original inhabitants of Cuba, the Taino Indians, smoked crude "cigars" made from rolled tobacco leaf. Today, this Caribbean island is widely acknowledged as still being the producer of the finest cigars and cigar tobacco in the world.

The finest tobacco is produced in the Vuelta Abajo province of Pinar del Rio, near the towns of San Luis and San Juan y Martinez. The climatic and soil conditions in this part of Cuba are perfect for the growing of tobacco, and it is the only region that produces all the leaves needed to blend a cigar. The province's annual rainfall of over 152cm (60in) a year is one of the highest on the island. The main growing period is between November and February, the dry season, when temperatures average 27°C (81°F) with eight hours of sunshine a day and average humidity of 64%. The

LEFT: An 18th-century print of Havana harbour, as used on a cigar box.

tobacco is grown on many privately owned smallholdings that sell the product at a fixed price to the Communist government. After the revolution of 1959, most of the cultivated land was seized from the international tobacco companies that were mainly American-owned, and peasants, or *vegueros*, now cultivate the patchwork of smallholdings, ranging in size from 2 hectares (5 acres) to a maximum of 60 hectares (150 acres).

Other areas in Cuba that grow fine tobacco leaf are Semi Vuelta, also in the province of Pinar del Rio, the Partidos area close to Havana, Remedios, in the centre of the island and Oriente at the eastern end.

In the mid-19th century there were nearly 10,000 tobacco plantations in Cuba and over

BELOW: The Partagas factory in downtown Havana.

BELOW: Curing barns, where tobacco leaf is left to dry.

ABOVE: Wrapper leaves are hung to air-dry in a curing barn.

few years, Cuba has exported between 50 and 80 million handmade cigars in 22 brands annually – as against around 30 million just after the revolution.

After the revolution the names of the famous Havana factories were changed: La Corona became Fernando Roig; Partagas, Francisco Perez German; El Rey del Mundo, Heroes del Moncada; and the best-known of all, Romeo Y Julieta, became Briones Montoto. However, the old names are still displayed outside the 19th- and early 20th-century Spanish-style factory buildings. Each factory concentrates on the manufacture of a number of brands of a particular flavour. For example, the Partagas, Gloria Cubana, Bolivar and Ramon Allones brands are all made in the old 1845 Partagas factory, which manufactures nearly 5 million cigars a year.

First-class Cuban brands include the very full-bodied Bolivar, the superb Cohiba, the superior Diplomaticos, the rare and mild Gispert, the superior H. Upmann and Hoyo de Monterrey, to name but a few. Generally, Havana cigars have a medium to full-bodied taste, with coffee, honeyed and earthy tones.

1,000 cigar factories situated in Havana and other large cities. At the beginning of the 20th century there were around 120 factories making over 200 brands of cigar in Cuba, and cigar-makers became the core of the Cuban industrial working class. After the revolution, a large proportion of Cuba's leading tobacco and cigar producers fled to other countries, such as the Canary Islands and the Dominican Republic, where many have flourished.

Many claimed that the quality of Havana cigars fell after the revolution, but the Cubans responded by introducing Montecristo and Cohiba cigars, the world's most sought after premium brands. Today, there are only six factories making handmade cigars in Cuba, but production has increased sharply. Over the last

BELOW: Workers in the Partagas factory open bunches of dried wrapper leaf.

BOLIVAR

Bolivar cigars were introduced in 1901 by the Rocha Company of Havana. They are named after Simon Bolivar, one of the great romantic figures of the 19th century, who liberated much of South America from oppressive Spanish rule. Although a large range of Bolivar cigars is hand-made, there are also some machine-made versions available. The flavour of the reasonably priced handmade cigars is full, and they are therefore not recommended for the novice cigar smoker. However, the machine-bunched range is not so strong in flavour and is therefore more suitable for the beginner. There is also a separate range of Bolivar cigars made in the Dominican Republic.

FROM LEFT TO RIGHT: *Corona Gigante, Corona Extra, Belicoso Fino, Corona Junior.*

NAME	SIZE	RING GAUGE
Corona Gigante	17.8cm/7in	47
Churchill	17.8cm/7in	47
Palma	17.8cm/7in	33
Immensa	17cm/6¾in	43
Lonsdale	16.8cm/6⅝in	43
Gold Medal Lonsdale	16.2cm/6⅜in	42
Corona Extra	14.3cm/5⅝in	44
Belicoso Fino	14cm/5½in	52
Corona	14cm/5½in	42
Petit Corona	12.7cm/5in	42
Bonita	12.7cm/5in	40
Royal Corona	12.4cm/4⅞in	50
Regente	12.4cm/4⅞in	34
Corona Junior	10.8cm/4¼in	42
Demi-Tasse	9.8cm/3⅞in	30
CEDAR-LINED TUBES		
Churchill	17.8cm/7in	47
Tubos No. 1	14cm/5½in	42
Tubos No. 2	12.7cm/5in	42
Tubos No. 3	12.4cm/4⅞in	34
MACHINE-BUNCHED SERIES		
Champion	14cm/5½in	40
Panetela	12.7cm/5in	35
Chicos	10.6cm/4³⁄₁₆in	29

ABOVE: *Bolivar Churchill and cedar-lined tube.*

LEFT: *The Bolivar motif from the inside of the cigar box.*

COHIBA

For centuries, historians have speculated on what the name *cohiba* meant to the Cuban Indians of Columbus's time. Some were of the opinion that *cohiba* was a name used for a pipe; others thought it referred to the tobacco plant. It is now known that *cohiba* was the term used for a bunch of tobacco leaves roughly rolled together to form something that we would call a cigar.

The Cohiba brand was created in 1966 as Havana's premier brand, for diplomatic use only. The story goes that Castro's bodyguard had a private supply of cigars which he purchased from a local *tobacquero*. Castro enjoyed the taste of

the cigars so much that he secretly installed their maker, Eduardo Ribera, in a Havana mansion, so that he could make them exclusively for the government.

From 1982 the brand was offered to the general public in three sizes: Lancero, Corona Especiale and Panetela. Three more sizes were added in 1989 – Esplendido, Robusto and Exquisito – to complete La Linea Clasica. Then in 1992 the five sizes of La Linea 1492 were announced: Siglo I, II, III, IV and V. The flavour of La Linea Clasica is medium to full, while La Linea 1492 is medium.

Robusto

ABOVE LEFT: Siglo II
ABOVE RIGHT: Exquisito

Cohiba tobaccos are grown on only ten selected *vegas*, or plantations, in the Vuelta Abajo region. The pick of the crop is selected from the five best *vegas* producing, in any year, each type of leaf required to make a Cohiba cigar. Availability will always be limited, because nothing is allowed to compromise the Cohiba brand's supremely high standards. Filler tobaccos used for Cohiba cigars benefit from an additional fermentation in cedar casks. This lasts for up to two years and further enhances the delicacy of the tobacco's flavour. It brings to Cohiba a taste that stands out, even in the illustrious company of Havana's other *Grandes Marques*.

Only the most skilful cigar rollers in Cuba are allowed to make Cohibas and, to ensure a perfect result every time, each Cohiba roller specializes in making just one size. Every stage of production is strictly monitored by a highly qualified quality-control team, which is the custodian of the legendary Cohiba aroma and flavour. All finished cigars are checked for weight, girth and shape. Samples of each roller's work are smoked every week, to ensure they satisfy the company's demanding standards for flavour, draw and combustion.

LEFT: *Each box of Cohibas is carefully colour-matched.*

RIGHT: *Panetela*

NAME	SIZE	RING GAUGE
LA LINEA CLASICA SERIES		
Lancero	19cm/7½in	38
Esplendido	17.8cm/7in	47
Coronas Especiale	15.2cm/6in	38
Exquisito	12.7cm/5in	36
Robusto	12.4cm/4⅞in	50
Panetela	11.4cm/4½in	26
LA LINEA 1492 SERIES		
Siglo V	16.8cm/6⅝in	43
Siglo IV	14.3cm/5⅝in	46
Siglo III	15.5cm/6⅛in	42
Siglo II	12.7cm/5in	42
Siglo I	10.2cm/4in	40

FROM LEFT TO RIGHT: Lancero, Esplendido, Siglo V, Siglo III, Siglo IV.

Extra care is taken to colour-match the cigars in each box of Cohibas. They are graded into no less than 80 shades, with a predominance of light- to mid-*claro* tones, and some of a golden *colorado* hue. A range of Cohiba cigars, made in the Dominican Republic by General Cigar, should not be confused with these superb Havanas.

CUABA

The Habanos Corporation introduced the Cuaba brand of mild to medium, handmade cigars to the market in 1996. This new brand recreates a style that was popular at the end of the 19th century and its *figuardos vitolas* were designed especially for smokers who appreciate antiquity. The name Cuaba is very old. The word, like Cohiba, came from the Taino Indians, the original inhabitants of Cuba. It described a special kind of bush, still grown on the island, that burns so well that it was used to light the cigars or *cohibas* during religious ceremonies. Its use was first chronicled in the early 16th century: *"Quemar como una Cuaba"* ("To burn like a Cuaba"). This Cuban expression passed down over the centuries and is still in use today, particularly among farmers.

ABOVE: *The Cuaba brand was launched in 1996, but the style of cigar harks back to the 19th century.*

RIGHT: *Exclusivo*
FAR RIGHT: *Tradicionale*

NAME	SIZE	RING GAUGE
Exclusivo	14.3cm/5⅝in	46
Generoso	13.3cm/5¼in	42
Tradicionale	12cm/4¾in	42
Divino	10.2cm/4in	43

During the 19th century, Havanas with shapely bodies tapering to a point, in a form known as *figuardos*, were the height of fashion. Smaller sizes, too, were popular for enjoyment during intervals at the opera. Gradually, in the 20th century, the fashion changed to *parejos* or straight-sided cigars, and by the late 1930s *figuardos* had virtually disappeared. The new Cuaba *figuardos* are made in the Romeo Y Julieta factory, which has a long tradition of making this style of cigar.

BELOW: Generoso
BOTTOM: Divino

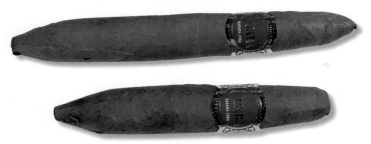

DIPLOMATICOS

This range of superior, medium- to full-bodied, handmade cigars was introduced to the French market in the 1960s, as a lower-priced alternative to Montecristo. The range comes in seven sizes and availability is somewhat limited, but the cigars represent good value for money. The design of the Diplomaticos cigar band, a horse-drawn carriage, has been widely copied by the Dominican manufacturer of Licenciados cigars.

NAME	SIZE	RING GAUGE
No. 1	16.5cm/6½in	42
No. 2	15.5cm/6⅛in	52
No. 3	14cm/5½in	42
No. 4	12.7cm/5in	42
No. 5	10.2cm/4in	40
No. 6	19cm/7½in	38
No. 7	15.2cm/6in	38

EL REY DEL MUNDO

El Rey del Mundo, or "King of the World", was launched so successfully in 1882 by the Antonio Allones factory, that it was soon renamed the El Rey del Mundo Cigar Company. These popular, handmade cigars are now produced in the Romeo Y Julieta factory in Havana, and the flavour of this large range is light to medium.

NAME	SIZE	RING GAUGE
Grande de Espana	19.2cm/7^9/$_{16}$in	38
Taino	17.8cm/7in	47
Elegante	17.5cm/6^7/$_8$in	28
Lonsdale	16.2cm/6^3/$_8$in	42
Gran Corona	14cm/5^1/$_2$in	46
Corona de Luxe	14cm/5^1/$_2$in	42
Choix Supreme	12.7cm/5in	48
Petit Corona	12.7cm/5in	42
Très Petit Corona	11.4cm/4^1/$_2$in	40
Lunch Club	10.2cm/4in	42
Demi-Tasse	9.8cm/3^7/$_8$in	30

LEFT: *Choix Supreme*   RIGHT: *Lonsdale*

FLOR DE CANO

The company of J. Cano was founded in 1884 by Tomas and José Cano. Against the trend for larger companies, they remained small and independent until the Cuban revolution. Their name lives on in this small selection of light- to medium-flavoured, handmade cigars.

NAME	SIZE	RING GAUGE
Diademas	17.8cm/7in	47
Selectos	14.6cm/5^3/$_4$in	41
Gran Corona	14.3cm/5^5/$_8$in	46
Corona	12.7cm/5in	42
Predilecto Tubulare	12.7cm/5in	42
Short Churchill	12.4cm/4^7/$_8$in	50

HOYO DE MONTERREY

Sr. José Gener grew tobacco in the Vuelta Abajo village of San Juan y Martinez prior to the founding of his brand of cigars in 1865. Hoyo de Monterrey is one of the oldest brands still in existence. The handmade cigars are medium in flavour, while the Le Hoyo series was introduced in the 1970s, in response to the demand for a richer tasting cabinet range.

BELOW: Des Dieux from the Le Hoyo series.

FROM LEFT TO RIGHT: Double Corona, des Dieux, du Dauphin, du Roi, du Prince, Churchill.

ABOVE FROM LEFT TO RIGHT: Du Gourmet, Epicure No.1, Epicure No. 2, du Deputé, du Maire.

	SIZE	RING GAUGE
Double Corona	19.4cm/7⅝in	49
Churchill	17.8cm/7in	47
Jeanne D'Arc	14.3cm/5⅝in	35
Corona	14cm/5½in	42
Short Corona	12.7cm/5in	42
Margarita	12cm/4¾in	26
LE HOYO SERIES (SLIDE-LID BOX)		
Le Hoyo du Gourmet	16.8cm/6⅝in	33
Le Hoyo des Dieux	15.2cm/6in	42
Le Hoyo du Dauphin	15.2cm/6in	38
Le Hoyo du Roi	14cm/5½in	42
Le Hoyo du Prince	12.7cm/5in	40
Le Hoyo du Deputé	10.8cm/4¼in	38
Le Hoyo du Maire	9.8cm/3⅞in	30
CABINET SELECTION (SLIDE-LID BOX)		
Epicure No. 1	14.3cm/5⅝in	46
Epicure No. 2	12.4cm/4⅞in	50

H. UPMANN

Originally a banker, Herman Upmann became so fond of the cigars that were sent to him from Cuba, that he moved to Havana in 1844. There he continued banking and set up as a cigar-maker. The cigar company was taken over by Frankau & Company in 1922. A further change of ownership came about in the mid-1930s, when it was purchased by the company of Menendez y Garcia. Each box of H. Upmann cigars still carries the signature of Herman Upmann.

LEFT: *Sir Winston*, BELOW LEFT: *Grand Corona*, BELOW RIGHT: *Petit Upmann*

NAME	SIZE	RING GAUGE
Sir Winston	17.8cm/7in	47
Seleccion Suprema	17.8cm/7in	33
Upmann No. 1	16.5cm/6½in	42
Cinco Bocas	16.5cm/6½in	42
Upmann No. 2	15.5cm/6⅛in	52
Grand Corona	14.6cm/5¾in	40
Amatista	14.6cm/5¾in	40
Culebras	14.6cm/5¾in	39
Super Corona	14cm/5½in	46
Corona	14cm/5½in	42
Royal Corona	14cm/5½in	42
Cristales	13.5cm/5⁵⁄₁₆in	42
Kings	12.9cm/5¹⁄₁₆in	42
Petit Corona	12.7cm/5in	42
No. 4	12.7cm/5in	42
Petit Upmann	11.5cm/4½in	36
CABINET SELECTION		
Magnum (Slide-lid Box)	14cm/5½in	46
Connoisseur No. 1 (Slide-lid Box)	12.7cm/5in	48
CEDAR-LINED TUBES		
Monarch	17.8cm/7in	47
Corona Major	12.7cm/5in	42
Corona Minor	11.7cm/4⅝in	40
Corona Junior	11.4cm/4½in	36

LA GLORIA CUBANA

These superior-quality, medium- to full-flavoured, handmade cigars were reintroduced in the 1970s and are produced in the Partagas factory in Havana. The limited quantity Medaille d'Or range is supplied in beautifully varnished 8-9-8 boxes.

BELOW: The famous Partagas factory manufactures La Gloria Cubana brand.

NAME	SIZE	RING GAUGE
Especial (Semi Boite Nature)	19cm/7½in	38
Especial No. 2 (Semi Boite Nature)	15.2cm/6in	38
Joyita (Semi Boite Nature)	11.4cm/4½in	26
No. 1	16.5cm/6½in	42
No. 2	15.5cm/6⅛in	52
No. 3	14cm/5½in	42
No. 4	12.7cm/5in	42
No. 5	10.2cm/4in	40
CEDAR-LINED TUBES		
Tubo	15.2cm/6in	42
Petit Tubo	12.7cm/5in	42

MONTECRISTO

Montecristo was introduced in 1935 by the H. Upmann factory. The brand appeared originally in only five sizes, described by number. Other sizes like the A and Especiales were added in the early 1970s. The brand is named after the novel by Alexandre Dumas, *The Count of Montecristo*, and the boxes are decorated with an attractive fleur-de-lis and crossed sword.

Montecristo's distinctive flavour has made it one of the most popular Havana brands for over 20 years. It is the best-selling Havana cigar, accounting for nearly 50% of all handmade cigars exported, with a large proportion going to Spain, France, the UK and Switzerland. The flavour is medium to full.

FROM LEFT TO RIGHT: No. 1, No. 2, No. 3, No. 4, No. 5.

FROM LEFT TO RIGHT: *Joyita, Especial No. 2, Especial, A.*

BELOW: *The Montecristo logo is one of the best-known of the Cuban cigars.*

NAME	SIZE	RING GAUGE
A	24cm/9½in	47
Especial	19cm/7½in	38
Especial No. 2	15.2cm/6in	38
Tubos	15.2cm/6in	42
Joyita	11.4cm/4½in	26
No. 1	16.5cm/6½in	42
No. 2	15.2cm/6in	38
No. 3	14cm/5½in	42
No. 4	12.7cm/5in	42
No. 5	10.2cm/4in	42

PARTAGAS

Don Jaime Partagas founded his factory in Havana in 1845. Apart from the period from 1987 to 1990, when the building was being restored, the cigars are still made at this famous factory. This well-known brand of full-flavoured cigars still retains its rich blend of tobaccos. The large range includes many machine-bunched, hand-finished and machine-made examples. A range of Partagas cigars is also handmade in the Dominican Republic and is recognized by the year "1845" printed on the band.

FROM LEFT TO RIGHT: Lusitania,
Partagas 8-9-8 (varnished),
Partagas 8-9-8 (unvarnished),
Corona, Petit Corona.

*ABOVE AND RIGHT: The lining (above)
and lid (right) of the Partagas box.*

LEFT: Series D No. 4
RIGHT: Très Petit Corona

NAME	SIZE	RING GAUGE
Lusitânia	19.4cm/7⅝in	49
Series du Connoisseur No. 1	19.2cm/7⁹⁄₁₆in	36
Churchill De Luxe	17.8cm/7in	47
Palme Grande	17.8cm/7in	33
Partagas de Partagas No. 1	17cm/6¾in	43
Seleccion Privada No. 1	17cm/6¾in	43
Partagas 8-9-8 (Varnished)	17cm/6¾in	43
Lonsdale	16.5cm/6½in	42
Presidente	15.5cm/6⅛in	47
Partagas 8-9-8 (Unvarnished)	15.2cm/6in	42
Corona Grande	15.2cm/6in	42
Culebra	14.4cm/5¹¹⁄₁₆in	39
Corona	14cm/5½in	42
Charlotte	14cm/5½in	35
Petit Corona	12.7cm/5in	42
Series D No. 4 (Semi Boite Nature)	12.4cm/4⅞in	50
Très Petit Corona	11.4cm/4½in	40
Short	10.8cm/4¼in	42
Chico	10.5cm/4⅛in	29

POR LARRANAGA

The oldest Havana cigar still in production, originally introduced in 1834, Por Larranaga cigars are not widely available. Smartly dressed in reddish, oily wrappers, they are of a superior quality, with a medium- to full-bodied flavour. The cigar is mentioned in Rudyard Kipling's poem *The Betrothed*: "There's peace in a Larranaga, there's calm in a Henry Clay". The range of cigars also includes machine-made examples.

BELOW: The old and much-loved Por Larranaga brand features in the writings of Rudyard Kipling. Today, they are available in extremely limited numbers.

NAME	SIZE	RING GAUGE
Lonsdale	16.5cm/6½in	42
Lancero	14.1cm/5⁹⁄₁₆in	42
Corona	14cm/5½in	42
Petit Corona	12.9cm/5¹⁄₁₆in	42
Coronita	12.7cm/5in	38
Nectare No. 4	11.6cm/4⁹⁄₁₆in	40
Small Corona	11.5cm/4½in	40

PUNCH

The Punch brand was founded in 1840 by Don Manuel Lopez of J. Valle & Company and is one of the oldest still being produced today. The name was adopted with the British market in mind, at a time when the humorous magazine, *Punch*, was extremely popular. The familiar character of Mr Punch, smoking a cigar, is still featured on the labels of each box.

The large range of superior-quality cigars, some of which are machine-made, is of medium flavour and reasonably priced. Confusingly, there is also a superior-quality range of Punch cigars made in Honduras.

LEFT: Petit Corona

RIGHT: Double Corona

BELOW: The design on the lining paper of the cigar box features the famous Punch character. The brand was aimed specifically at the British market.

NAME	SIZE	RING GAUGE
Diadema	24cm/9½in	47
Double Corona	19.4cm/7⅝in	49
Churchill	17.8cm/7in	47
Panetela Grande	17.8cm/7in	33
Super Selection No. 1	15.5cm/6⅛in	42
Black Prince	14.3cm/5⅝in	46
Punch Punch	14.3cm/5⅝in	46
Seleccion de Luxe No. 1	14.3cm/5⅝in	46
Corona	14cm/5½in	42
Royal Coronation	14cm/5½in	42
Presidente	12.7cm/5in	42
Petit Corona	12.7cm/5in	42
Margarita	12cm/4¾in	26
Petit Coronation	11.4cm/4½in	40
Coronet	11.4cm/4½in	34
Punchinello	11.4cm/4½in	34
Très Petit Corona	10.8cm/4¼in	42
Petit Punch	10.2cm/4in	40
CEDAR-LINED TUBES		
Churchill	17.8cm/7in	47
Coronation	12.7cm/5in	42
Petit Coronation	11.4cm/4½in	40
Coronet	11.4cm/4½in	34

*ABOVE FROM LEFT TO RIGHT:
Churchill, Punch Punch,
Corona.*

ABOVE: The Punch cigar band.

*RIGHT: Another lining paper design
pays homage to the brand's founder,
Manuel Lopez.*

MANUEL LOPEZ

QUINTERO

Augustin Quintero opened a small factory in the 1920s in Cienfuegos, near the Remedios tobacco-growing region in the centre of Cuba. The success of his cigars enabled him to found, with his eldest brother, the Quintero y Hermano company in Havana in 1940. These light-flavoured cigars, with their delicate blend of Vuelta Abajo tobaccos, are ideal for a first introduction to Havanas. Some of the Quintero range of cigars are machine-made and appear in the same sizes as the hand-made range.

RIGHT AND BELOW: Although now manufactured in Havana, Quintero packaging makes reference to the company's origins in Cienfuegos.

NAME	SIZE	RING GAUGE
Churchill	16.5cm/6½in	42
Corona	14cm/5½in	42
Nacionale	14cm/5½in	40
Panetela	12.7cm/5in	36
Londres Extra	12.7cm/5in	40
Purito	10.8cm/4¼in	29
CEDAR-LINED TUBES (HAND-FINISHED)		
Tubulare	12.7cm/5in	36

RIGHT: Panetela

RAFAEL GONZALEZ

This range of superior-quality, mild-flavoured, handmade cigars was introduced in 1928 for the British market and is now manufactured in the Romeo Y Julieta factory in Havana. The cedarwood box is printed with the following instructions: "These cigars have been manufactured from a secret blend of pure Vuelta Abajo tobaccos, selected by the Marquez Rafael Gonzalez, Grandee of Spain. For more than twenty years this brand has existed. In order that the Connoisseur may fully appreciate the perfect fragrance, they should be smoked either within one month of the date of shipment from Havana, or should be carefully matured for about one year."

FROM LEFT TO RIGHT: *Lonsdale, Petit Corona, Très Petit Lonsdale, Corona Extra.*

NAME	SIZE	RING GAUGE
Slenderella	17.5cm/6⁷⁄₈in	28
Lonsdale (Vitola "B")	16.2cm/6³⁄₈in	42
Corona Extra	14.3cm/5⁵⁄₈in	46
Petit Corona	12.8cm/5¹⁄₁₆in	42
Petit Lonsdale	12.7cm/5in	42
Panetela Extra	12.7cm/5in	37
Panetela	11.7cm/4⁵⁄₈in	34
Très Petit Lonsdale (Vitola "H")	11.4cm/4¹⁄₂in	40
Cigaritto	11.4cm/4¹⁄₂in	26
Demi-Tasse	10.2cm/4in	30

RAMON ALLONES

This brand of superior-quality, full-bodied, mainly handmade cigars was founded by a Spaniard, Ramon Allones, in 1837. Allones was the first cigar manufacturer to use attractive labelling on his cigar boxes, in this case the coat of arms  of the Spanish royal family. The cigars, the second oldest in production in Cuba, have been made in the Partagas factory since the 1920s. There are a few machine-made examples also available. A milder range of Ramon Allones is also manufactured in the Dominican Republic.

RIGHT: Ramon Allones packaging makes use of the coat of arms of the Spanish royal family.

FROM LEFT: Petit Corona, Small Club Corona.

NAME	SIZE	RING GAUGE
Gigante	19.4cm/7⅝in	49
Churchill 8-9-8	17cm/6¾in	43
Topper	15.2cm/6in	40
Corona 8-9-8	14.3cm/5⅝in	42
Petit Corona	12.7cm/5in	42
Panetela	12.7cm/5in	35
Allones Specially Selected	12.4cm/4⅞in	50
Ramonita	12.4cm/4⅞in	26
Small Club Corona	11.1cm/4⅜in	42

ROMEO Y JULIETA

Romeo Y Julieta was founded by Alvarez y Garcia in 1875 and purchased by Fernandez Rodriguez in 1903. Rodriguez travelled widely, raced his horse Julieta in Europe and produced many thousands of personalized, one-off cigar bands for the royalty and celebrities of the day. The attractive labelling on the cigar boxes depicts the famous balcony scene from Shakespeare's play *Romeo and Juliet*. The extremely large range of superior-quality cigars, both handmade and machine-made, is medium in flavour. Superior-quality handmade cigars of the same name are also produced in the Dominican Republic.

NAME	SIZE	RING GAUGE
Fabuloso	24cm/9½in	47
Clemenceau	17.8cm/7in	47
Prince of Wales	17.8cm/7in	47
Shakespeare	17.5cm/6⅞in	28
Cedro de Luxe No. 1	16.5cm/6½in	42
Cazadore	16.2cm/6⅜in	44
Corona Grande	15.2cm/6in	42
Belicoso	14cm/5½in	52
Exhibicion No. 3	14cm/5½in	46
Cedro de Luxe No. 2	14cm/5½in	42
Corona	14cm/5½in	42
Petit Corona	12.7cm/5in	42
Romeo No. 2 de Luxe	12.9cm/5¹/₁₆in	42
Exhibicion No. 4	12.7cm/5in	48
Cedro de Luxe No. 3	12.7cm/5in	42
Panetela	11.7cm/4⅝in	34
Très Petit Corona	11.4cm/4½in	40
Petit Prince	10.2cm/4in	40
Petit Julieta	10.2cm/4in	30
CEDAR-LINED TUBES		
Churchill	17.8cm/7in	47
No. 1	14cm/5½in	42
No. 2	12.7cm/5in	42
No. 3	11.5cm/4½in	40

ABOVE: *The distinctive red and gold band of Sir Winston Churchill's favourite cigar.*

ABOVE FROM LEFT TO RIGHT: *Prince of Wales, Corona, Cedro de Luxe No. 3, Cedro de Luxe No. 2, Churchill.*

MADE IN HABANA, CUBA

ABOVE: The balcony scene from Romeo and Juliet. *Legend has it that this was one of the cigar-makers' favourite plays, which gave name to this popular and well-respected brand.*

BELOW FROM TOP TO BOTTOM: Petit Prince, Petit Corona, Exhibicion No. 4.

SAINT LUIS REY

This range of superior-quality, full-bodied, handmade cigars is among the best Havana cigars available. They were introduced in the 1940s and are named after the American film, *The Bridge of Saint Luis Rey*, based on the book by Thornton Wilder. The cigars, made in the Romeo Y Julieta factory in Havana, and packed in smartly designed, white boxes, are only available in limited numbers but, conversely, are reasonably priced. They are not to be confused with the similarly named San Luis Rey cigars from Germany, which are machine-made.

BELOW: Series A

BOTTOM: Petit Corona

NAME	SIZE	RING GAUGE
Double Corona	19.4cm/7⅝in	49
Churchill	17.8cm/7in	47
Lonsdale	16.5cm/6½in	42
Series A	14.3cm/5⅝in	46
Corona	14.3cm/5⅝in	42
Petit Corona	12.8cm/5¹/₁₆in	42
Regios	12.7cm/5in	48

SANCHO PANZA

This small range of superior-quality, mild-flavoured, handmade cigars has only been available in Spain until recently. It is popular with some aficionados as a daytime cigar.

ABOVE: Non Plus

BELOW LEFT AND RIGHT: The box lining depicts the character from Cervantes' famous novel, Don Quixote.

Name	Size	Ring gauge
Sancho	23.5cm/9¼in	47
Corona Gigante	17.8cm/7in	47
Molino	16.5cm/6½in	42
Dorado	16.5cm/6½in	42
Panetela Largo	16.5cm/6½in	28
Corona	14.3cm/5⅝in	42
Belicoso	14cm/5½in	52
Non Plus	12.7cm/5in	42
Bachillere	11.6cm/4⁹⁄₁₆in	40

TRINIDAD

The rarest brand in the world, the Trinidad is only produced in one size. It is thought by some that Fidel Castro has them made to give as personal gifts to visiting heads of state. This superb-quality, medium- to full-bodied cigar is handmade at the El Laguito factory in Havana. From early 1998 there were plans to make this coveted cigar available to the general public.

NAME	SIZE	RING GAUGE
Trinidad	19cm/7½in	38

RIGHT: Trinidad

VEGAS ROBAINA

Vegas Robaina is a completely new brand of handmade cigars introduced by Habanos S.A. in 1997. Initially only available in Spain, the brand will soon be sold throughout the world. It is named after Don Alejandro Robaina, the head of a renowned Cuban tobacco-growing family. Sr. Robaina has been running their plantations since 1950 and his family's tradition goes back to the mid-19th century. The brand, produced at the H. Upmann factory in Havana, is totally handmade, with filler from the San Luis area of the Vuelta Abajo and the wrapper from the famous Vega Alejandro.

NAME	SIZE	RING GAUGE
Don Alejandro	19.3cm/7⅝in	49
Clasico	16.5cm/6½in	42
Unico	15.5cm/6⅛in	52
Familiar	14cm/5½in	42
Famoso	12.7cm/5in	48

THE DOMINICAN REPUBLIC

The Dominican Republic occupies the eastern two-thirds of the island of Hispaniola in the West Indies. The remaining third is Haiti. Since its discovery by Christopher Columbus in 1492, it has been ruled by a mixture of Spanish, French and Haitians.

The earliest recorded mention of Dominican tobacco concerns Thomas Warner who, in 1622, established tobacco plantations on the north of the island, on behalf of various English companies. Throughout the 18th century tobacco production flourished, with Santiago de los Caballeros the centre of the industry. Spain purchased all the produce of its American colonies, and this policy of monopoly state purchase was also applied to Hispaniola. However, unlike other colonies which were under complete Spanish control, Hispaniola was partially occupied by the French, and the north-west coast was used as a

ABOVE: *Tobacco fields in Santiago de los Caballeros.*

BELOW: *Young tobacco plants, one week after planting.*

base by pirates and smugglers. Tobacco producers from the Cibao region preferred to sell their tobacco at market prices to the French and to smugglers. The Cibao producers rarely exported even the minimum quota of tobacco that the Spanish guaranteed to purchase, nor could they declare this "contraband" production, as it was illegal for them to trade with any other country. Dominican tobacco sold in this way was therefore branded as originating from other countries.

The Dominican Republic has had an unstable history. The Spanish ceded the country to France and it was then incorporated into

Haiti. Dominica engaged in wars of liberation against the Haitians.

During this period it was independent for nearly 50 years, prior to declaring its own independence in 1844, whereupon the Haitian invasions recommenced. The US army occupied the country from 1914 to 1924, and again in 1965. The Dominican Republic has been ruled by a number of dictators, notably Trujillo (1930–1961), who virtually made tobacco production his own state monopoly.

Tobacco production suffered greatly until after Trujillo's assassination, when, in 1962, the Instituto del Tabaco was formed and immediately set about placing the manufacturing of tobacco on a more professional basis. It selected the best native varieties of tobacco plants and introduced new varieties, the most notable being Piloto Cubano. By selecting appropriate seeds, the Instituto del Tabaco created a technological base that improved the systems of cultivation and production then in place. It then set about stabilizing production.

Throughout the 18th and 19th centuries there was much mass emigration from Dominica to Cuba. The emigrants took with them the tools of their trade, including their farmed tobacco seeds. After the Cuban Revolution of 1959, this was repeated in reverse and Cuban manufacturers introduced their native tobacco seeds into other tobacco-growing countries.

No other country has been able to produce tobacco from Cuban seed, of the same quality

LEFT: Arturo Fuente produces the incredibly rare Fuente Fuente Opus X® in the Dominican Republic.

as the Dominican Republic. It is thought the present Cuban tobacco is the result of partial, unscientific hybridization with Dominican tobacco over the last two centuries. When this tobacco seed was returned to Dominica after 1959, it found growing conditions that were peculiarly suitable. Such is the quality of the seed tobacco that the Dominican Republic exports it to other premium cigar-producing countries, such as Honduras, Jamaica, Mexico, Nicaragua, the USA, and also to Cuba itself.

The Dominican Republic is now the world's biggest producer of premium cigars, which are made entirely by hand. In 1996 it exported 139 million premium cigars to the USA alone, more than the next four top countries put together, and 48% of the total US imports of

BELOW: The Dominican Instituto del Tabaco has improved methods of cultivation, ensuring consistently good-quality, high-yield crops.

ABOVE: Cigar-making at the Rothmans factory. The Dominican Republic is the world's biggest producer of handmade cigars.

premium cigars during 1996. Estimates for the total 1996 Dominican exports are in excess of 250 million premium cigars.

The boom in cigar production in the Dominican Republic started slowly following the USA embargo on Cuban products. At first, there was an increase in demand for tobacco grown in the country, to be exported as leaf to the USA. However, as the production costs for machine-made cigars in the USA rose, and became higher than those in the Dominican Republic for hand-rolled cigar products, more Dominican manufacturers started to introduce their own brands into the world markets.

Some Dominican brands have the same names as the famous Cuban ones. Other first-class Dominican brands include Arturo Fuente, Avo, Casa Blanca, Davidoff, Dunhill, Valdrych, Santa Damiana and Paul Garmirian. Dominican cigars are by far the most popular in the USA and have a mild, sweet taste.

Until recently only filler tobacco was grown in the Dominican Republic. The wrappers and binders were imported from Cameroon, Honduras, Brazil, Mexico, Ecuador and the USA. In recent years wrappers have been successfully grown in the Dominican Republic, notably on the Fuente family's plantation.

ARTURO FUENTE

The Fuente family originally came from Cuba. The first Fuente, Arturo, emigrated to Tampa, Florida, where he set up the Fuente factory. He was succeeded by his son, Carlos Sr. In 1980 a factory was established in the Dominican Republic with seven employees. Now the family employs 1,800 people in six factories in Santiago, and is run by Carlos Fuente Sr and his son, Carlos Fuente Jr. They are the largest producers of handmade cigars in the country, turning out over 24 million cigars every year.

NAME	SIZE	RING GAUGE
Canone	21.6cm/8½in	52
Royal Salute	19cm/7½in	52
Churchill	19cm/7½in	48
Panetela Fina	17.8cm/7in	38
Double Corona	17cm/6¾in	48
Privada No. 1	17cm/6¾in	46
Corona Imperial	16.5cm/6½in	46
Lonsdale	16.5cm/6½in	42
Flor Fina	15.2cm/6in	46
Cuban Corona	13.3cm/5¼in	44
Petit Corona	12.7cm/5in	38
Epicure	11.5cm/4½in	50
Chico	10cm/4in	32
RESERVA SUPERIOR LIMITADA		
No. 3	13.7cm/5½in	40
No. 4	12.7cm/5in	38
Don Carlos	12.7cm/5in	50
OPUS X® SERIES		
Reserva A	23.5cm/9¼in	47
Double Corona	19.3cm/7⅝in	49
Reserva No. 1	16.8cm/6⅝in	44
Reserva No. 2	16cm/6¼in	52
Petit Lancero	16cm/6¼in	38
Fuente Fuente	14.3cm/5⅝in	46
Robusto	13.3cm/5¼in	50

ABOVE LEFT: No. 4
ABOVE RIGHT: Chico

The company uses a blend of four different types of tobacco for its filler and has pioneered the production of wrapper leaves in the Dominican Republic. These have been used on the Fuente Fuente Opus X® series, which was launched in 1995. The production of these cigars is extremely limited, although the company has extended its tobacco plantations next door to the Château de la Fuente farm in El Caribe which, it is hoped, will double the production of this series. Apart from these cigars, the Fuentes produce a standard range and the Hemingway series of large *figuardos*. The cigars are mainly made using rare *colorado* Cameroon wrappers, although some use natural Connecticut Shade wrappers. They are well-made and blended, with a light to medium flavour. The Fuente brand is one of the most popular in the USA.

FROM LEFT TO RIGHT: Double Corona, Panetela Fina, Petit Corona, Reserva Superior Limitada No. 4, Epicure.

ASHTON

These are choice, handmade cigars, named after their creator, William Ashton Taylor, an English pipe-maker. They are now produced by an American-owned company. The cigars, all wrapped in Connecticut leaf with Cuban-seed Dominican binder, are produced in three different styles with distinct flavours: Ashton, Ashton Aged Cabinet Selection and Ashton Aged Maduro. Due to extra ageing, the Cabinet Selection is the mildest. The Aged Maduro, using broad-leaf wrappers, gives a mellow smoke with a sweet flavour.

FROM LEFT TO RIGHT: Magnum, Corona, Panetela, 8-9-8.

NAME	SIZE	RING GAUGE
ASHTON		
Churchill	19cm/7½in	52
Prime Minister	17.5cm/6⅞in	48
8-9-8	16.5cm/6½in	44
Elegante	16.5cm/6½in	35
Double "R"	15.2cm/6in	50
Panetela	15.2cm/6in	36
Corona	14cm/5½in	44
Cordial	12.7cm/5in	30
Magnum	12.7cm/5in	50
ASHTON AGED CABINET SELECTION		
Cabinet No. 1	23cm/9in	52
Cabinet No. 7	16cm/6¼in	52
Cabinet No. 10	19cm/7½in	52
Cabinet No. 8	17.8cm/7in	50
Cabinet No. 2	17.8cm/7in	46
Cabinet No. 3	15.2cm/6in	46
Cabinet No. 6	14cm/5½in	50
ASHTON AGED MADURO		
No. 60	19cm/7½in	52
No. 50	17.8cm/7in	48
No. 30	17cm/6¾in	44
No. 40	15.2cm/6in	50
No. 20	14cm/5½in	44
No. 10	12.7cm/5in	50

AVO

This superior brand of handmade cigars was created in 1986 by the American musician, Avo Uvezian, writer of the hit song "Strangers in the Night". The cigars are all handmade with Connecticut wrapper and Cuban-seed Dominican binders and fillers. The more expensive XO series undergoes a longer ageing process than the standard range.

FROM LEFT TO RIGHT: No. 2, No. 3, No. 4, No. 6, No. 8.

NAME	SIZE	RING GAUGE
No. 3	19cm/7½in	52
Pyramid	17.8cm/7in	54
No. 4	17.8cm/7in	38
No. 5	17cm/6¾in	46
No. 1	17cm/6¾in	42
No. 6	16.5cm/6½in	36
No. 2	15.2cm/6in	50
Belicoso	15.2cm/6in	50
No. 7	15.2cm/6in	44
No. 8	14cm/5½in	40
No. 9	12cm/4¾in	48
Petit Belicoso	11.5cm/4½in	50
XO SERIES		
Maestoso	17.8cm/7in	48
Preludo	15.2cm/6in	40
Intermezzo	14cm/5½in	50

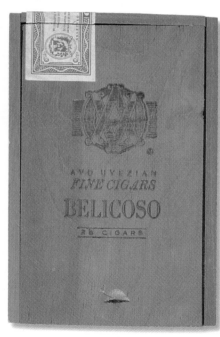
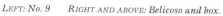

LEFT: *No. 9*   RIGHT AND ABOVE: *Belicoso and box.*

COHIBA

These cigars were developed by the General Cigar Company in the 1980s to take advantage of the reputation of the legendary Cohiba cigars made in Cuba. The filler is a blend of properly aged tobaccos from the Dominican Republic, with a Jember binder and a Connecticut wrapper. The taste is full-bodied, and the cigars continue to mature in cedar boxes once made.

ABOVE: The Dominican brand of Cohiba cigars, named after the renowned Cuban brand, is made from a blend of tobaccos grown in the Dominican Republic.

NAME	SIZE	RING GAUGE
Robusto	12.7cm/5in	49
Churchill	17.8cm/7in	49
Corona Especiale	16.5cm/6½in	42
Lonsdale Grande	15.9cm/6¼in	47
Robusto Fino	12cm/4¾in	47
Corona	13cm/5⅛in	42
Corona Minor	10.2cm/4in	42
Crystal Corona	14cm/5½in	42
Triangulo	15.2cm/6in	54

ABOVE FROM LEFT TO RIGHT:
Robusto, Corona, Corona Especiale,
Lonsdale Grande, Churchill.

LEFT: *Corona Minor*

CUESTA-REY

Cuesta-Rey produces three series of superior-quality, handmade cigars – Cabinet Selection, Centennial Collection and No. 95 – in the Dominican Republic. The company was originally founded in Tampa, Florida, in 1884 by Angel La Madrid Cuesta, and the cigars were made from Cuban tobacco imported into the USA. The Centennial Collection, created to celebrate the company's centenary, is made with light Connecticut wrappers and Dominican binders, the Cabinet Selection with Connecticut broad-leaf wrappers, and No. 95 with *colorado* Cameroon wrappers.

ABOVE: *The Cuesta-Rey label illustrates the numerous prizes awarded the brand.*

FROM LEFT TO RIGHT: *Aristocrat, Captiva and tube, Dominican No.4, Centennial Collection No. 3.*

BELOW: *A box of Cuesta-Rey Dominican No. 3.*

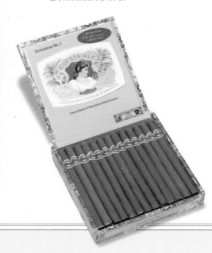

NAME	SIZE	RING GAUGE
CABINET COLLECTION		
No. 1	21.6cm/8½in	52
No. 2	17.8cm/7in	36
No. 95	15.9cm/6¼in	42
No. 898	17.8cm/7in	49
No. 1884	16.5cm/6½in	44
CENTENNIAL COLLECTION		
Individual	21.6cm/8½in	52
Dominican No. 1	21.6cm/8½in	52
Dominican No. 2	18.4cm/7¼in	48
Dominican No. 3	17.8cm/7in	36
Dominican No. 4	16.5cm/6½in	42
Dominican No. 5	14cm/5½in	43
Dominican No. 7	11.4cm/4½in	50
Aristocrat	18.4cm/7¼in	48
Captiva	15.7cm/6³⁄₁₆in	42
Cameo	10.8cm/4¼in	32

FROM LEFT TO RIGHT: No. 5, No. 7 Maduro, No. 7, Cameo, No. 1, No. 1 Maduro.

DAVIDOFF

Zino Davidoff was born in Russia, where his father ran a tobacconist's shop. In 1911 the Davidoff family emigrated to Switzerland and opened a tobacco shop in Geneva. After travelling to South and Central America in the 1920s, Zino ended up in Cuba, where he formed an affectionate relationship with the country that lasted until 1990. After World War II he

FROM LEFT TO RIGHT:
Thousand series: 5000, 4000,
3000, 2000, 1000.

NAME	SIZE	RING GAUGE
Ambassadrice	11.5cm/4½in	26
ANNIVERSARIO SERIES		
No. 1	22.1cm/8¹¹⁄₁₆in	48
No. 2	17.8cm/7in	48
GRAND SERIES		
Grand Cru No. 1	15.5cm/6⅛in	42
Grand Cru No. 2	14.3cm/5⅝in	42
Grand Cru No. 3	12.7cm/5in	42
Grand Cru No. 4	11.7cm/4⅝in	40
Grand Cru No. 5	10.2cm/4in	40
SPECIAL SERIES		
Double R	19cm/7½in	50
Special R	12.7cm/5in	50
Special T	15.2cm/6in	52
THOUSAND SERIES		
1000	11.7cm/4⅝in	34
2000	12.7cm/5in	42
3000	17.8cm/7in	33
4000	15.5cm/6⅛in	42
5000	14.3cm/5⅝in	46
Tubos	15.2cm/6in	38

created his Château selection, based on the Cuban Hoyo de Monterrey brand.

In the early 1970s Zino Davidoff formed a partnership with Ernst Schneider, a major Swiss cigar importer, and Cubatabaco, and

ABOVE: Davidoff Tubos

together they successfully marketed three series of Havana cigars throughout the world. In 1990, because of a dispute between Cubatabaco and Schneider's Oettinger Imex company, production of the three series of Davidoffs ceased in Cuba and manufacture was moved to the Dominican Republic. The cigars are now made with *claro* Connecticut wrappers and, although they are among the best cigars produced in Dominica, they are different from the Davidoffs previously produced in Cuba – the overall flavour is lighter.

FROM LEFT TO RIGHT: *Grand Series: Grand Cru No. 1, Grand Cru No. 2, Grand Cru No. 3, Grand Cru No. 4, Grand Cru No. 5.*

LEFT AND RIGHT: *Davidoff cigars are among the best produced in the Dominican Republic.*

FROM LEFT TO RIGHT: *Special T, Special R, Ambassadrice, Anniversario No.2, Anniversario No. 1.*

LEFT: *Davidoff accessories include a wide range of premium cigar cutters.*

DON DIEGO

Originally made in the Canary Islands until the 1970s, this excellent range of handmade cigars uses either Connecticut or Cameroon wrappers, with a Dominican filler and binder. The cigars are made in the Tabacalera de Garcia factory in La Romana for Consolidated Cigar Corporation. Certain sizes are available in either American Market Selection (AMS), double *claro* or English Market Selection (EMS), *colorado* wrappers. These cigars are much appreciated among aficionados and beginners alike for the mild taste.

NAME	SIZE	RING GAUGE
Corona Brava	16.5cm/6½in	48
Corona EMS/AMS	14.3cm/5⅝in	42
Grande	15.2cm/6in	50
Grecos EMS	16.5cm/6½in	38
Lonsdale EMS/AMS	16.8cm/6⅝in	42
Petit Corona EMS/AMS	13cm/5⅛in	42
TUBED CIGARS		
Corona Major Tube EMS	12.8cm/5¹⁄₁₆in	42
Monarch Tube EMS	18.4cm/7¼in	46
Royal Palm Tube EMS	15.5cm/6⅛in	36
SMALL CIGARS		
Babies	12.8cm/5¹⁄₁₆in	33
Prelude EMS	10.2cm/4in	28

LEFT: *Lonsdale, Grande, Royal Palm*
RIGHT: *Corona*

DON JUAN PLATINUM

These medium- to full-bodied cigars are a handmade speciality of Tropical Tobacco Inc. in the Dominican Republic. The cigars have a creamy and smooth character, and are made with a Connecticut Shade wrapper, Dominican binder and a Nicaraguan and Dominican filler.

NAME	SIZE	RING GAUGE
Presidente	21.6cm/8½in	50
Churchill	17.8cm/7in	49
Numero Uno	16.8cm/6⅝in	44
Torpedo	15.2cm/6in	52 or 30
Matador	15.2cm/6in	50
Cetro	15.2cm/6in	43
Linda	14cm/5½in	38
Robusto	12.7cm/5in	50

LEFT TO RIGHT: Matador, Robusto, Churchill.

DUNHILL

Dunhill's range of superior-quality, handmade cigars has been manufactured in the Dominican Republic since 1989. For the Dunhill Aged cigars three types of leaf are used: Dominican Piloto, Olor and Brazil. These provide the constituents of the filler and binder; the wrapper is Connecticut Shade. These cigars, distinguished by the blue-and-white Dunhill band, are made from tobacco taken from a single year and are aged in cedar-lined rooms for three months. The properties of the cedarwood allow the aroma and flavour to achieve a subtle balance. A smaller, separate range of Dunhill cigars, recognizable by their black-and-white bands, is made in the Canary Islands.

FROM LEFT TO RIGHT: *Tabaras and tube, Caleta,*
Bavaro, Romana.

NAME	SIZE	RING GAUGE
DUNHILL AGED SERIES		
Peravia	17.8cm/7in	50
Cabreras	17.8cm/7in	48
Fantino	17.8cm/7in	28
Diamante	16.8cm/6⅝in	42
Samana	16.5cm/6½in	38
Centena	15.2cm/6in	50
Condado	15.2cm/6in	48
Panetela	15.2cm/6in	30
Tabaras	14.1cm/5⁹⁄₁₆in	42
Valverde	14cm/5½in	42
Altamiras	12.7cm/5in	48
Romana	11.4cm/4½in	50
Bavaro	11.4cm/4½in	28
Caleta	10.2cm/4in	42

FROM LEFT TO RIGHT:
Altamiras and tube,
Valverde, Cabreras
and tube.

FROM LEFT TO RIGHT: *Peravia, Fantino, Diamante,*
Samana, Condado, Panetela, Senorita.

FONSECA

Fonseca cigars have been made in the Dominican Republic since 1965, although a small range is still made in Cuba. These superior-quality Dominican cigars are handmade using Connecticut wrappers, Mexican binders and Dominican fillers. The cigars are well-made, with a light to medium flavour.

ABOVE: The simple yet distinctive Fonseca logo is stamped on to the lid of every box.

FROM LEFT TO RIGHT: 5-50, 7-9-9, 10-10, Triangular.

NAME	SIZE	RING GAUGE
10-10	17.8cm/7in	50
7-9-9	16.5cm/6½in	46
8-9-9	15.2cm/6in	43
Triangular	14cm/5½in	56
5-50	12.7cm/5in	50
2-2	10.8cm/4¼in	40

THE GRIFFIN'S

This small range of superior-quality and expensive handmade cigars, now solely distributed by Davidoff, has been manufactured in the Dominican Republic for some years. The cigars are made with a Connecticut wrapper and Dominican filler and binder.

NAME	SIZE	RING GAUGE
Prestige	19cm/7½in	50
Privilege	12.7cm/5in	32
No. 100	17.8cm/7in	38
No. 200	17.8cm/7in	43
No. 300	15.9cm/6¼in	43
No. 400	15.2cm/6in	38

FROM LEFT TO RIGHT: *Prestige, No. 200, No. 100, No. 300.*

BELOW: *The mythical griffin appears on all boxes and labels.*

H. UPMANN

H. Upmann, a member of a respected European banking family, opened a cigar factory in Cuba in 1844. After several changes of ownership in 1922 and 1935, the brand is still made in Havana. In more recent times, good-quality Upmann handmade cigars have also been manufactured at the La Romana factory of Tabacalera de Garcia in the Dominican Republic for the Consolidated Cigar Corporation. Until recently the wrappers were Cameroon, but have since been replaced by Indonesian. The binder and filler is Dominican. To differentiate between Dominican and Cuban Upmanns, the labels are marked "H. Upmann 1844" and "H. Upmann Habana" respectively.

FROM LEFT TO RIGHT: *Pequenos No. 100, Robusto, Tubo, Naturale Tube, Lonsdale.*

NAME	SIZE	RING GAUGE
Churchill	19.4cm/7^5/$_8$in	46
Corona Imperiale	17.8cm/7in	46
Corona	14.1cm/5^9/$_{16}$in	42
Corona Brava	16.5cm/6^1/$_2$in	48
El Prado	17.8cm/7in	36
Lonsdale	16.8cm/6^5/$_8$in	42
No. 2000 SBN	17.8cm/7in	42
Petit Corona	12.8cm/5^1/$_{16}$in	42
Pequenos No. 100	11.4cm/4^1/$_2$in	50
Pequenos No. 200	11.4cm/4^1/$_2$in	46
Pequenos No. 300	11.4cm/4^1/$_2$in	42
TUBED CIGARS		
Corona Major Tube	12.8cm/5^1/$_{16}$in	42
Tubo Gold Tube	12.8cm/5^1/$_{16}$in	42
Extra Finos Gold Tube	17cm/6^3/$_4$in	38
Finos Gold Tube	15.5cm/6^1/$_8$in	36
Monarch Tube	17.8cm/7in	46
Naturale Tube	15.5cm/6^1/$_8$in	36
Corona Cristal	14.1cm/5^9/$_{16}$in	42
Panetela Cristal	17cm/6^3/$_4$in	38
CABINET SELECTION		
Columbo	20.3cm/8in	50
Corsario	14cm/5^1/$_2$in	50
Robusto	12cm/4^3/$_4$in	50
SMALL CIGARS		
Demi-Tasse	11.4cm/4^1/$_2$in	33
Aperitif	10.2cm/4in	28

BELOW: No. 2000 SBN

HENRY CLAY

These cigars are named after an early 19th-century American congressman and secretary of state, who had business connections with Cuba. They were made in Havana until the 1930s when, for a brief period, the manufacturing moved to New Jersey, USA. The small range of good-quality cigars are now handmade at the Tabacalera de Garcia factory in La Romana for the Consolidated Cigar Corporation, using Connecticut broadleaf wrapper and Dominican filler and binder. The smooth taste is good for a beginner, with different blends created for US and European markets. The boxes still carry the attractive colour picture of the original Henry Clay factory in Havana.

FROM TOP TO BOTTOM: *Brevas Finas, Brevas ala Conserva, Brevas.*

NAME	SIZE	RING GAUGE
Brevas Finas	16.5cm/6½in	48
Brevas ala Conserva	14.3cm/5⅝in	46
Brevas	14cm/5½in	42

JUAN CLEMENTE

Founded by Frenchman Jean Clement in 1982, this company produces fewer than half a million cigars a year, making them difficult to find. The cigars are handmade with Connecticut leaf wrappers, a Dominican binder and a mix of four fillers. This combination of fillers results in a uniquely varied taste. The band is located at the foot of the cigar, holding a protective silver-paper wrapping in place.

FROM LEFT TO RIGHT: Panetela, Corona, Rothschild, Demi-Corona.

NAME	SIZE	RING GAUGE
Especiale	19cm/7½in	38
Churchill	17.5cm/6⅞in	46
Panetela	16.5cm/6½in	34
Grand Corona	15.2cm/6in	42
Corona	12.7cm/5in	42
No. 530	12.7cm/5in	30
Rothschild	12.4cm/4⅞in	50
Demi-Corona	10.2cm/4in	40
CLUB SELECTION		
No. 1	15.2cm/6in	50
No. 2	11.4cm/4½in	46
No. 3	17.8cm/7in	44
No. 4	14.6cm/5¾in	42

*RIGHT: Club Selection No. 2,
Club Selection No. 4. The Club Selection series
is aged for 4 years, and offers a more robust
blend than others in the Juan Clemente range.*

*BELOW: When Jean Clement began producing
these cigars in 1982, he used the Spanish
version of his name for the brand.*

KISKEYA

These mild-flavoured cigars are handmade in the Dominican Republic by Tropical Tobacco Inc. They are made with a Dominican filler, Dominican Havana-seed binder and Ecuadorean Connecticut-seed wrapper. They are available with both natural and *maduro* wrapping.

FROM TOP TO BOTTOM: Churchill, No. 1, Rothschild.

NAME	SIZE	RING GAUGE
Viajante	21.6cm/8½in	52
Presidente	19cm/7½in	50
Churchill	17.8cm/7in	48
No. 1	17cm/6¾in	44
Palma Fina	17.8cm/7in	36
Cetro	15.9cm/6¼in	44
Toro	15.2cm/6in	50
No. 2	15.2cm/6in	42
No. 4	14cm/5½in	42
Rothschild	12.7cm/5in	50

LICENCIADOS

These superior-quality cigars have been handmade in the Dominican Republic since 1990. The two series of Licenciados cigars are graced by a band bearing the stage-coach emblem, identical to the Cuban brand, Diplomaticos. The cigars are made with Connecticut wrappers and a blend of Dominican filler. These cigars are mild in flavour.

NAME	SIZE	RING GAUGE
Soberano	21.6cm/8½in	52
Presidente	20.3cm/8in	50
Panetela	17.8cm/7in	38
Excelente	17cm/6¾in	43
Toro	15.2cm/6in	50
Licenciados No. 4	14.6cm/5¾in	43
Wavell	12.7cm/5in	50
SUPREME RANGE		
500	20.3cm/8in	50
400	15.2cm/6in	50
300	17cm/6¾in	43
200	14.6cm/5¾in	43

FROM TOP TO BOTTOM: Supreme 400, Licenciados No. 4, Wavell.

ABOVE RIGHT: Supreme 500

MACANUDO

These superior-quality, handmade cigars, one of the most popular brands in the USA, were first made in Jamaica in 1868. They are now manufactured by the General Cigar Company, both in Jamaica and in the Dominican Republic. The same blends are used in each location and it is extremely difficult to differentiate between the countries of origin. Apart from the Vintage Range, made only in Jamaica, they all use Connecticut Shade wrappers, grown on the company's farms in the Connecticut valley, Mexican binders and a blend of Jamaican, Mexican and Dominican fillers.

Macanudo cigars offer a rich, complex flavour with an exceptionally smooth smoke. They are consistently well-made and deserve their high reputation.

RIGHT: A box of Macanudo Prince Philip.

NAME	SIZE	RING GAUGE
Prince of Wales	20.3cm/8in	52
Prince Philip	19cm/7½in	49
Portofino	17.8cm/7in	34
Baron de Rothschild	16.5cm/6½in	42
Duke of Windsor	15.2cm/6in	50
Claybourne	15.2cm/6in	31
Hampton Court	14.6cm/5¾in	43
Crystal	14cm/5½in	50
Hyde Park	14cm/5½in	49
Duke of Devon	14cm/5½in	42
Petit Corona	12.7cm/5in	38
Ascot	10.6cm/4³⁄₁₆in	32
Caviar	10.2cm/4in	36
Miniature	9.5cm/3¾in	24

FROM LEFT TO RIGHT: *Prince of Wales,*
Baron de Rothschild, Crystal,
Duke of Devon, Duke of Windsor,
Hyde Park, Prince Philip Maduro.

RIGHT: *A box of Prince Philip*
Maduro cigars.

MACANUDO VINTAGE

These are also made by the General Cigar Company. Occasionally a tobacco harvest yields a small quantity of exceptional filler, binder and wrapper leaves. These few leaves are given the appellation of "Vintage" and are used to roll Macanudo Vintage Cabinet Selection cigars. The years 1979, 1984, 1988 and 1993 all produced tobacco of this quality, and in the summer of 1996 the first issue of the 1993 vintage crop was released. Macanudo Vintage cigars are identified by the imprint of the year of the vintage on the box and band of each cigar. All cigars have two bands, the red Macanudo Vintage band and a separate, second band showing the vintage from which it came. The leaves are aged more gradually than other tobaccos, and the cigars are incomparably smooth to smoke. The price of these cigars reflects the scarcity and age of the vintage.

FROM LEFT TO RIGHT: Vintage I, Vintage II, Vintage III, Vintage IV.

BELOW: Macanudo Vintage Cabinet selection IV, packaged in a slide-lid cedar box.

NAME	SIZE	RING GAUGE
No. I	19cm/7½in	49
No. II	16.7cm/6⁹/₁₆in	43
No. III	14.1cm/5⁹/₁₆in	43
No. IV	11.4cm/4½in	47

MONTECRISTO

Not to be confused with the popular cigars of the same name that have been made in Cuba since 1935, this is a more recent brand produced in the Dominican Republic for sale in the USA. The range of seven handmade cigars, apart from the Robusto, all use an American wrapper with a filler and binder from the Dominican Republic. The Robusto uses a wrapper from Cameroon, with a filler and binder from Brazil and the Dominican Republic. The cigars are made at the La Romana factory of Tabacalera de Garcia for the Consolidated Cigar Corporation.

NAME	SIZE	RING GAUGE
Churchill	17.8cm/7in	48
No. 1	16.5cm/6½in	44
Double Corona	15.9cm/6¼in	50
No. 2 (Torpedo)	15.2cm/6in	50
No. 3	14cm/5½in	44
Corona Grande	13.3cm/5¼in	46
Robusto	10.8cm/4¼in	50

RIGHT: Robusto

BELOW: Montecristo cigars, named after the famous Cuban brand, are handmade in the Dominican Republic for the Consolidated Cigar Corporation.

FROM LEFT TO RIGHT: *Churchill,
No. 1, Double Corona, No. 2, No. 3.*

MONTECRUZ

The Menendez family originally made the Montecristo brand in Cuba. Following the Castro Revolution of 1959, the family moved to the Canary Islands, where it started making the Montecruz brand. This operation was moved to the Dominican Republic in the 1970s and these superior-quality cigars are now handmade by the Consolidated Cigar Corporation. The cigars, produced in the Dominican Republic since 1977, are known as "Montecruz Sun Grown". They use Cameroon wrappers with a filler combining Brazilian and Dominican tobaccos and a Dominican binder. A milder range of cigars, using Connecticut wrappers – the Natural Claro Line – is also produced by the company for Dunhill.

NAME	SIZE	RING GAUGE
Individuale	20.3cm/8in	50
Colossus	16.5cm/6½in	50
Tubulare	15cm/1⅛in	36
Cedar-Aged	12.7cm/5in	42
Junior	12.4cm/4⅞in	33
Robusto	11.5cm/4½in	50
Chico	9.8cm/3⅞in	28
Montecruz F	18.4cm/7¼in	47
Montecruz D	17.8cm/7in	36
Montecruz A	16.8cm/6⅝in	43
No. 200	18.4cm/7¼in	46
No. 201	15.5cm/6⅛in	38
No. 205	17.8cm/7in	42
No. 210	16.5cm/6½in	42
No. 220	14cm/5½in	42
No. 240	12cm/4¾in	44
No. 250	16.5cm/6½in	38
No. 255	17.8cm/7in	36
No. 265	14cm/5½in	38
No. 270	12cm/4¾in	35
No. 280	17.8cm/7in	33
No. 281	15.2cm/6in	33
No. 282	12.7cm/5in	42

FROM LEFT TO RIGHT: *Tubulare, Colossus, Junior, Robusto, Cedar-Aged, No.200.*

MONTESINO

This small range of good quality, mild- to medium-flavoured, handmade cigars is manufactured by Arturo Fuente using Cuban-seed Dominican wrappers.

NAME	SIZE	RING GAUGE
Napoleon Grande	17.8cm/7in	46
No. 1	17.5cm/6⅞in	43
No. 3	17cm/6¾in	36
Fuma	17cm/6¾in	44
Gran Corona	17cm/6¾in	48
No. 2	15.9cm/6¼in	44
Cesar No. 2	15.9cm/6¼in	44
Diplomatico	14cm/5½in	42

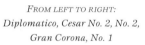

FROM LEFT TO RIGHT:
Diplomatico, Cesar No. 2, No. 2,
Gran Corona, No. 1

NAT SHERMAN

The Nat Sherman tobacco empire, founded in the 1930s and centred on its world-famous shop on Fifth Avenue, in Manhattan, produces an extensive range of handmade Dominican cigars. The distinctive bands carry the emblem of the famous Nat Sherman clock, which dominates the shop front. Different-coloured bands are used to identify each selection, which are all named after the Sherman family or an aspect of New York life.

FROM LEFT TO RIGHT: *Metropolitan Selection: Metropolitan, Nautical, University, Explorer, Angler.*

The Exchange, Gotham and V.I.P. selections all use Connecticut wrappers, the Landmark selection uses Cameroon wrappers, and the Manhattan and City Desk selections use Mexican wrappers. The Exchange selection has a mild, smooth flavour; the Landmark selection a more full-bodied taste, while the Gotham selection provides a mild smoke. The vast range of Nat Sherman cigars truly provides something for everyone, due to its different combinations of filler, wrapper and binder.

FROM LEFT TO RIGHT: V.I.P. Selection: Morgan, Carnegie, Astor.
Gotham Selection: No. 65, No. 711, No. 1400, No. 500.

NAME	SIZE	RING GAUGE
METROPOLITAN SELECTION		
Metropolitan	17.8cm/7in	47 or 60
Nautical	17.8cm/7in	34 or 48
University	15.2cm/6in	50
Explorer	14cm/5½in	44 or 56
Angler	14cm/5½in	43
V.I.P. SELECTION		
Morgan	17.8cm/7in	42
Zigfeld Fancytail	17cm/6¾in	38
Carnegie	15.2cm/6in	48
Astor	11.4cm/4½in	50
CITY DESK SELECTION		
Tribune	19cm/7½in	50
Dispatch	16.5cm/6½in	46
Telegraph	15.2cm/6in	50
Gazette	15.2cm/6in	42
HOST SELECTION		
Harrington	19cm/7½in	47
Hampton	17.8cm/7in	50
Hunter	17cm/6¾in	43
Hudson	15.2cm/6in	34
Hobart	14cm/5½in	49
Hamilton	14cm/5½in	42

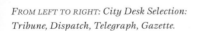

FROM LEFT TO RIGHT: City Desk Selection: Tribune, Dispatch, Telegraph, Gazette.

RIGHT: A box of Nat Sherman cigars from the Host selection, one of the few from the Nat Sherman range that use a Honduran binder and filler.

NAME	SIZE	RING GAUGE
MANHATTAN SELECTION		
Gramercy	17cm/6¾in	43
Chelsea	16.5cm/6½in	38
Tribeca	15.2cm/6in	31
Sutton	14cm/5½in	49
Beekman	13.3cm/5¼in	28
GOTHAM SELECTION		
No. 500	17.8cm/7in	50
No. 1400	15.9cm/6¼in	44
No. 711	15.2cm/6in	50
No. 65	15.2cm/6in	32
EXCHANGE SELECTION		
Butterfield No. 8	16.5cm/6½in	42
Trafalgar No. 4	15.2cm/6in	47
Murray Hill No. 7	15.2cm/6in	38
Academy No. 2	12.7cm/5in	31
LANDMARK SELECTION		
Algonquin	17cm/6¾in	43
Vanderbilt	15.2cm/6in	47
Metropole	15.2cm/6in	34
Hampshire	14cm/5½in	42

ABOVE FROM LEFT TO RIGHT: Landmark Selection: Vanderbilt, Hampshire, Metropole, Algonquin

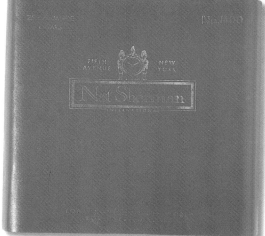

RIGHT: The Gotham selection is packaged in a dark green box, embellished with the famous Nat Sherman clock.

ONYX

This small range of good-quality, handmade, mild cigars was introduced in the early 1990s. They use a Java binder, Dominican and Mexican filler and Mexican *maduro* wrapper.

NAME	SIZE	RING GAUGE
No. 852	20.3cm/8in	52
No. 750	19cm/7½in	50
No. 646	16.8cm/6⅝in	46
No. 642	15.2cm/6in	42
No. 650	15.2cm/6in	50

FROM LEFT TO RIGHT: No. 852, No. 750, No. 642, No. 650.

OSCAR

Introduced in the 1980s, this small range of excellent handmade cigars caters for most tastes. In size, they cover the spectrum from the Oscarito cigarillo to the giant Don Oscar. They all use a mix of Dominican fillers and binders with a Connecticut wrapper.

NAME	SIZE	RING GAUGE
Don Oscar	23cm/9in	46
Supreme	20.3cm/8in	48
No. 700	17.8cm/7in	54
No. 200	17.8cm/7in	44
No. 100	17.8cm/7in	38
No. 300	15.9cm/6¼in	44
No. 400	15.2cm/6in	38
No. 500	14cm/5½in	50
Prince	12.7cm/5in	30
No. 600	11.4cm/4½in	50
Oscarito	10.2cm/4in	20

FROM LEFT TO RIGHT: No.600, No.500, No.400, No. 700, No.200, Supreme

PARTAGAS

Partagas was founded in the mid-19th century in Cuba and the original factory in Havana still manufactures an extensive range of these well-known superior cigars. More recently, Partagas cigars have also been handmade in the Dominican Republic by the General Cigar Company. The two countries of origin can be recognized by the bands: the Dominican band is inscribed "Partagas 1845", the Cuban has "Habana".

The Partagas brand in the Dominican Republic is overseen by Ramon Cifuentes, who has spent a lifetime making Partagas cigars, initially in Cuba, before moving in the 1960s to the Dominican Republic. These cigars are made from Cameroon wrappers, a Mexican binder and a mix of Jamaican, Dominican and Mexican fillers. The finished cigars undergo a unique ageing process for three weeks in a room lined with Spanish cedar. They are then carefully colour-sorted and aged in boxes for another three months. The flavour is full-bodied and rich, with spicy notes and a touch of sweetness.

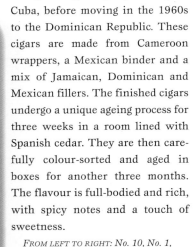

FROM LEFT TO RIGHT: No. 10, No. 1, Aristocrat, No. 2, Humitube.

BELOW: Partagas Robusto

NAME	SIZE	RING GAUGE
No. 10	19cm/7½in	49
Fabuloso	17.8cm/7in	52
8-9-8	17.5cm/6⅞in	44
Humitube	17cm/6¾in	43
No. 1	17cm/6¾in	43
Maduro	15.9cm/6¼in	48
Almirante	15.9cm/6¼in	47
Aristocrat	15.2cm/6in	50
No. 6	15.2cm/6in	34
Sabroso	14.9cm/5⅞in	44
No. 2	14.6cm/5¾in	43
Naturale	14cm/5½in	50
No. 4	12.7cm/5in	38
Robusto	11.4cm/4½in	49
Purito	10.6cm/4³⁄₁₆in	32
Miniatura	9.5cm/3¾in	24

RIGHT: Robusto, Naturale.

PARTAGAS LIMITED RESERVE

This range is produced by Ramon Cifuentes from the best Partagas Cameroon wrapper leaves, specially aged by a slower maturation process. Partagas claims that these cigars are aged more gradually and for longer periods of time than any other premium cigars. Each cabinet of cigars is accompanied by a certificate that indicates the year and month when the cigars were cedar-aged, packed and released, so the cigar aficionado can be assured of their quality.

LEFT: Epicure

NAME	SIZE	RING GAUGE
Royale	17cm/6¾in	43
Regale	15.9cm/6¼in	47
Robusto	14cm/5½in	49
Epicure	12.7cm/5in	38

PAUL GARMIRIAN

Founded in 1991 by the cigar aficionado, Paul Garmirian, the company makes some of the finest handmade cigars outside Havana. These superior-quality cigars are made with reddish-brown *colorado* wrappers and a Dominican binder and filler. They have a sweet and mellow taste and are only available in limited quantities.

LEFT TO RIGHT: No. 1, Lonsdale, Belicosa, Corona Grande.

NAME	SIZE	RING GAUGE
Celebration	23cm/9in	50
Double Corona	19.4cm/7⅝in	50
No. 1	19cm/7½in	38
Churchill	17.8cm/7in	48
Belicosa	16.5cm/6½in	52
Corona Grande	16.5cm/6½in	46
Lonsdale	16.5cm/6½in	42
Connoisseur	15.2cm/6in	50
Especial	14.6cm/5¾in	38
Belicoso Fino	14cm/5½in	52
Epicure	14cm/5½in	50
Corona	14cm/5½in	42
Robusto	12.7cm/5in	50
Petit Corona	12.7cm/5in	43
No. 2	12cm/4¾in	48
Petit Bouquet	11.4cm/4½in	38
No. 5	10.2cm/4in	40
Bombone	8.9cm/3½in	43

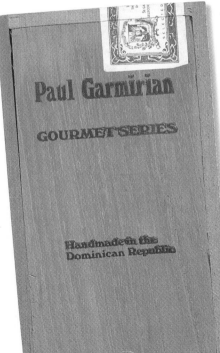

RIGHT: *Petit Bouquet,
Double Corona.*

LEFT: *The Paul
Garmirian range is
considered by
many to provide
the best quality
cigars outside
Havana.
Connoisseurs
expect to pay
accordingly.*

PLAYBOY BY DON DIEGO

This small range of English Market Selection (EMS) cigars is made at the La Romana factory of Tabacalera de Garcia for the Consolidated Cigar Corporation. The medium-bodied cigars have a Connecticut wrapper.

FROM LEFT TO RIGHT: Churchill, Gran Corona, Lonsdale, Double Corona, Robusto.

NAME	SIZE	RING GAUGE
Churchill EMS	19.7cm/7¾in	50
Gran Corona EMS	17cm/6¾in	48
Lonsdale EMS	16.5cm/6½in	42
Double Corona EMS	15.2cm/6in	52
Robusto EMS	12.7cm/5in	50

PLEIADES

This range of good-quality, mild cigars is handmade with Connecticut Shade leaf wrapper, Dominican binder and Olor and Piloto Cubano filler. The cigars are made in the Dominican Republic, then sent to France, where they are aged and packed at the company's facility in Strasbourg. The brand is owned by Swisher International. They are then exported throughout Europe and also back across the Atlantic to the USA. The cigars range from mild to rich and full-bodied, depending on the size chosen from the range of 12. The cedar boxes come complete with a built-in humidifier to keep these well-loved cigars in perfect condition.

Pleiades also produces a machine-made cigar, available only in the cigarillo size.

FROM TOP TO BOTTOM: *Orion, Mars.*

NAME	SIZE	RING GAUGE
Aldebran	21.6cm/8½in	50
Saturn	20.3cm/8in	46
Neptune	19cm/7½in	42
Sirius	17.5cm/6⅞in	46
Uranus	17.5cm/6⅞in	34
Orion	14.6cm/5¾in	42
Antares	14cm/5½in	40
Venus	13cm/5⅛in	28
Pluton	12.7cm/5in	50
Perseus	12.7cm/5in	34
Mars	12.7cm/5in	28

FROM LEFT TO RIGHT: *Neptune, Sirius Reserve Privée 1991,*
Sirius, Uranus, Pluton.

POR LARRANAGA

Not to be confused with the Cuban cigar of the same name, these superior-quality, handmade, Dominican cigars are made with Dominican binders, blended Brazilian and Dominican filler and Connecticut Shade leaf wrapper. The Cuban cigars have "Habana" printed on the band, while the Dominican bands are printed "La Romana".

Name	Size	Ring gauge
Fabuloso	17.8cm/7in	50
Cetro	17.5cm/6⁷⁄₈in	42
Delicado	16.5cm/6½in	36
Pyramid	15.2cm/6in	50
Nacionale	14.1cm/5⁹⁄₁₆in	42
Petit Cedro en Cedro	12.7cm/5in	38
Robusto	12.7cm/5in	50

FROM LEFT TO RIGHT: Pyramid, Robusto, Petit Cedro en Cedro, Nacionale, Delicado, Cetro, Fabuloso.

PRIMO DEL REY

This large range of handmade, superior-quality cigars is manufactured at the Tabacalera de Garcia factory in La Romana for the Consolidated Cigar Corporation. The Primo del Rey Club selection is identified by the elaborate gold-and-red band.

FROM TOP TO BOTTOM: Presidente, No.4.

NAME	SIZE	RING GAUGE
Seleccion No. 1	17.3cm/6¹³⁄₁₆in	42
Seleccion No. 3	17.3cm/6¹³⁄₁₆in	36
Presidente	17cm/6¾in	44
Chavon	16.5cm/6½in	41
Seleccion No. 2	15.9cm/6¼in	42
Reale	15.5cm/6⅛in	36
Cazadore	15.4cm/6¹⁄₁₆in	44
Seleccion No. 4	14cm/5½in	42
Panetela Extra	15.1cm/5¹⁵⁄₁₆in	34
Corto	10.2cm/4in	28
CLUB SELECTION		
Baron	21.6cm/8½in	52
Regal	17.8cm/7in	50
Aristocrat	17cm/6¾in	48
Noble	15.9cm/6¼in	44
GIFT PACK		
Royal Corona	15.2cm/6in	46
Lonsdale	16.5cm/6½in	42

RAMON ALLONES

Not to be confused with the Cuban brand of the same name, these excellent cigars, handmade by General Cigar in the Dominican Republic, have a mild to medium flavour. They are made with a Cameroon wrapper, Mexican binder and a filler that is a blend of Dominican, Mexican and Jamaican tobaccos. The Crystals are packed in individual glass tubes and the Trumps are packed in a cedar box without band or cellophane. Distribution is limited.

RIGHT: B, Crystal, Redondo.

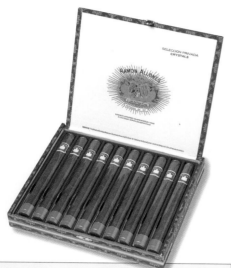

NAME	SIZE	RING GAUGE
Redondo	17.8cm/7in	49
A	17.8cm/7in	45
Trump	17cm/6¾in	43
Crystal	17cm/6¾in	42
B	16.5cm/6½in	42
D	12.7cm/5in	42

ROMEO Y JULIETA

One of the most famous cigar brands in the world, these superior, medium-bodied cigars are now handmade in the Dominican Republic, as well as Cuba. The Dominican cigars are made with a Cameroon wrapper, Connecticut broad-leaf binder and a Dominican and Cuban-seed filler. The excellent Vintage series, packed in a cedar box complete with humidifier, is made with a Connecticut Shade wrapper, an aged Mexican binder, and Dominican and Cuban-seed filler.

NAME	SIZE	RING GAUGE
VINTAGE SERIES		
Monarch	20cm/7⅞in	52
Presidente	17.8cm/7in	43
Delgado	17.8cm/7in	32
Romeo	15.2cm/6in	46
Palma	15.2cm/6in	43
Breva	14cm/5½ in	38
Panetela	13cm/5⅛in	35
Chiquita	10.8cm/4¼in	32

FROM LEFT TO RIGHT:

Palma, Chiquita, Monarch,

Presidente, Breva.

ROYAL DOMINICANA

This excellent range of mild- to medium-bodied cigars, handmade for J.R. Tobacco, is made with a Connecticut wrapper, Mexican binder and Dominican filler. The cigars are of excellent quality for their moderate price.

FROM LEFT TO RIGHT: Nacional, Super fino, Corona, No. 1, Churchill.

NAME	SIZE	RING GAUGE
Churchill	18.4cm/7¼in	50
No. 1	17cm/6¾in	43
Corona	15.2cm/6in	46
Super fino	15.2cm/6in	35
Nacional	14cm/5½in	43

ROYAL JAMAICA

This superior range of mild cigars was produced in Jamaica until 1989, when a hurricane flattened the crop and cigar factories. The extensive range was then handmade by the Consolidated Cigar Corporation in the Dominican Republic, using a Cameroon wrapper, a Java binder and a filler made from a blend of Dominican and Jamaican tobacco. From 1996, production began again in Jamaica, in addition to the Dominican manufacture. The *maduro* range is made with Brazilian wrappers, and a secret ingredient added during the fermentation process ensures the uniquely spicy flavour characteristic of Royal Jamaica.

ABOVE: *Gaucho*

NAME	SIZE	RING GAUGE
Goliath	23cm/9in	64
Churchill	20.3cm/8in	51
Giant Corona	19cm/7½in	49
Double Corona	17.8cm/7in	45
Doubloon	17.8cm/7in	30
Navarro	17cm/6¾in	34
Corona Grande	16.5cm/6½in	42
Rapier	16.5cm/6½in	28
Park Lane	15.2cm/6in	47
New York Plaza	15.2cm/6in	40
Royal Corona	15.2cm/6in	30
Buccaneer	14cm/5½in	30
Gaucho	13.3cm/5¼in	33
Robusto	11.4cm/4½in	49
Pirate	11.4cm/4½in	30
MADURO RANGE		
Churchill	20.3cm/8in	51
Corona Grande	16.5cm/6½in	42
Corona	14cm/5½in	40
Buccaneer	14cm/5½in	30

FROM LEFT TO RIGHT: *Corona,
Toro, Park Lane, Corona Grande,
Navarro, Churchill.*

SANTA DAMIANA

In the early years of the 20th century, the Santa Damiana brand, made in Cuba by the American Cigar Company, was popular both in the USA and the UK. In 1986 the Consolidated Cigar Corporation bought American Cigar and re-introduced the brand in 1992. The cigars are made in the modern Tabacalera de Garcia factory in the Duty Free Zone in the island's south-east corner, near Casa de Campo. The factory is one of the most sophisticated in the world with ultra-modern quality control.

Different blends and size names are used for the American Market Selection and English Market Selection brands. The USA sizes, called Seleccion No. 100, No. 700, and so on, contain a

FROM LEFT TO RIGHT: Corona, Petit Corona, Robusto, Torpedo.

lighter blend of tobaccos and have a milder flavour. The English brands have been evolved in conjunction with Hunters & Frankau of London, who have been cigar importers for over 200 years. These brands use the richer-tasting leaves from Dominican fillers and Connecticut Shade wrappers, and are designed for the smoker who prefers something more fully flavoured.

BELOW: The Santa Damiana brand uses Dominican-grown filler leaves for both its American and English market selection.

NAME	SIZE	RING GAUGE
AMERICAN MARKET SELECTION (AMS)		
Seleccion No. 800	17.8cm/7in	50
Seleccion No. 100	17cm/6¾in	48
Seleccion No. 700	16.5cm/6½in	42
Seleccion No. 300	14cm/5½in	46
Seleccion No. 500	12.7cm/5in	50
ENGLISH MARKET SELECTION (EMS)		
Churchill	17.8cm/7in	48
Torpedo	15.2cm/6in	52
Tubulare Extra	14cm/5½in	42
Corona	14cm/5½in	42
Robusto	12.7cm/5in	50
Petit Corona	12.7cm/5in	42
Tubulare	12.7cm/5in	42
Panetela	11.4cm/4½in	36

HONDURAS

The Republic of Honduras is a Central American country between Guatemala and Nicaragua. It has a damp, tropical climate with most of the rain falling in the north. The country once had a rich Mayan culture, reaching its peak in the 4th century. The tobacco plant, native to the country, was smoked by the Mayans for religious purposes. Discovered by Christopher Columbus in 1502, the country was soon conquered and settled by the Spanish, and remained under their control until 1821. Since then, frequent revolutions and army coups have marked its history.

In the early 1960s many Cuban émigré cigar producers left Cuba, after Castro's nationalization of the tobacco industry, and set up in Honduras. There has been major investment in the country by local and American tobacco companies, and the tobacco-growing and cigar-manufacturing industry has become increasingly important. Some Honduran brands have the same names as Cuban ones, for example El Rey del Mundo, Hoyo de Monterrey and Punch. Fine Honduran handmade cigars include Don Ramos, Don Tomas, Excalibur, La Invicta and Zino. Honduran cigars tend to have a spicy and robust taste. Although much of the tobacco is grown locally using Dominican, Connecticut and Cuban seed plants, some of the wrappers, binders and fillers are imported from Mexico, Nicaragua and the Dominican Republic.

Below: Tobacco fields in the Rio Copan valley.
The tobacco plant is native to Honduras.

BACCARAT HAVANA

This small range of reasonably priced, good-quality, full-bodied, handmade cigars is made with a Connecticut Shade leaf wrapper, Mexican binder and Honduran Cuban-seed filler. The special ingredients used to seal the cap add a sweet flavour to these cigars.

Name	Size	Ring gauge
Polo	17.8cm/7in	52
Churchill	17.8cm/7in	50
No. 1	17.8cm/7in	44
Luchadore	15.2cm/6in	43
Petit Corona	14cm/5½in	42
Rothschild	12.7cm/5in	50
Bonita	11.4cm/4½in	30

FROM LEFT TO RIGHT: Bonita, Rothschild, No. 1, Churchill.

BANCES

This brand was originally founded by Francisco Bances in the 1840s in Cuba. Following the Cuban Revolution, the company moved to Tampa, Florida, where machine-bunched cigars are still manufactured. These mild- to medium-flavoured Honduran cigars are handmade with a Honduran filler and a binder from Ecuador. They have spicy overtones and represent great value for money.

Name	Size	Ring gauge
Corona Immensa	17cm/6¾in	48
Cazadore	15.9cm/6¼in	44
El Prado	15.9cm/6¼in	36
Palma	15.2cm/6in	42
Breva	14cm/5½in	43
Unique	14cm/5½in	38

FROM LEFT TO RIGHT: *Palma, Breva, box of Brevas.*

BERING

This brand of cigars was founded in 1905 in Tampa, Florida. The machine-bunched cigars are now hand-rolled in Honduras by Swisher International. They are of excellent quality with a medium-bodied flavour.

NAME	SIZE	RING GAUGE
Grande	21.6cm/8½in	52
Immensa	18.1cm/7⅛in	45
Casinos	18.1cm/7⅛in	42
Baron	18.1cm/7⅛in	42
Torpedo	17.5cm/6⅞in	31 or 54
Cazadore	15.9cm/6¼in	45
Gold 1	15.5cm/6⅛in	33
Hispano	15.2cm/6in	50
Plaza	15.2cm/6in	43
Corona Royale	15cm/6in	41
Coronado (natural/candela)	13cm/5⅛in	45
Imperial	13cm/5⅛in	42
Robusto	11.8cm/4¾in	50

FROM LEFT TO RIGHT:
Robusto, Imperial
and tube, Coronado
Candela, Corona
Royale and tube.

FROM LEFT TO RIGHT: *Casino, Hispano, Gold 1, Cazadore, Torpedo, Immensa, Baron, Grande.*

LEFT: *Bering's Casino is packaged in a glass tube with a distinctive gold label.*

BERING
CASINOS
EXQUISITE CIGARS

C.A.O.

This range of good-quality, mild-flavoured, handmade cigars was intro-duced in 1994. The cigars are made with Connecticut Shade leaf wrappers, local binder tobacco and a filler of Mexican and Nicaraguan tobacco, pro-ducing a smooth, sweet taste.

NAME	SIZE	RING GAUGE
Churchill	20.3cm/8in	50
Presidente	19cm/7½in	54
Lonsdale	17.8cm/7in	44
Corona Gorda	15.2cm/6in	50
Corona	15.2cm/6in	42
Small Corona	12.7cm/5in	40
Robusto	11.4cm/4½in	50

FROM LEFT TO RIGHT:
Robusto, Corona Gorda,
Lonsdale, Churchill.

V CENTENNIAL

V Centennial are handmade in Honduras by Tropical Tobacco Inc. Selection, and processing of this range began in 1992. It was introduced in November 1993 to commemorate the Fifth Centennial anniversary of the discovery of America and of tobacco by Christopher Columbus. The superior-quality, medium- to full-bodied, handmade cigars are made with Mexican binder, a filler blended from Nicaraguan, Dominican and Honduran tobaccos and a Connecticut Shade leaf wrapper.

FROM LEFT TO RIGHT: Churchill, Torpedo, Cetro, Numero Dos, Robusto.

NAME	SIZE	RING GAUGE
Presidente	20.3cm/8in	50
Numero Uno	19cm/7½in	38
Torpedo	17.8cm/7in	36 or 54
Churchill	17.8cm/7in	48
Cetro	15.9cm/6¼in	44
Numero Dos	15.2cm/6in	50
Corona	14cm/5½in	42
Robusto	12.7cm/5in	50

CUBA ALIADOS

This large range of excellent-quality, medium-bodied, handmade cigars is produced in Honduras by Cuban émigré, Rolando Reyes. They are made with Ecuadorean Sumatran-seed wrappers, a Honduran binder, and Dominican and Brazilian filler. At 45.7cm (18in) long, with a ring gauge of 66, the General is the largest cigar currently made in the world.

NAME	SIZE	RING GAUGE
General	45.7cm/18in	66
Diadema	19cm/7½in	60
Piramide	19cm/7½in	60
Valentino	17.8cm/7in	48
Palma	17.8cm/7in	36
Corona de Luxe	16.5cm/6½in	45
Lonsdale	16.5cm/6½in	42
Toro	15.2cm/6in	54
No. 4	14cm/5½in	45
Rothschild	12.7cm/5in	51
Petit Cetro	12.7cm/5in	36

DON LINO

This extensive range of good-quality, mild to medium, handmade cigars was introduced in the late 1980s. The standard series is made with Honduran filler and a Connecticut Shade leaf wrapper. The Havana Reserve series is aged for four years and the recently introduced Colorado series has Connecticut broad-leaf wrappers.

NAME	SIZE	RING GAUGE
STANDARD SERIES		
Supremo	21.6cm/8½in	52
Churchill	19cm/7½in	50
Torpedo	17.8cm/7in	48
No. 3	15.2cm/6in	36
Corona	14cm/5½in	50
No. 4	12.7cm/5in	42
Rothschild	11.4cm/4½in	50
Epicure	11.4cm/4½in	32
COLORADO SERIES		
Presidente	19cm/7½in	50
Lonsdale	16.5cm/6½in	44
Robusto	14cm/5½in	50
HAVANA RESERVE SERIES		
Churchill	19cm/7½in	50
Torpedo	17.8cm/7in	48
Tubo	16.5cm/6½in	44
Toro	14cm/5½in	46
Robusto	12.7cm/5in	50
Rothschild	11.4cm/4½in	50
ORO SERIES		
Panetela	17.8cm/7in	36
No. 1	16.5cm/6½in	44
Toro	14cm/5½in	46

ABOVE FROM LEFT TO RIGHT: Oro No. 1, Colorado, Havana Reserve Tubo.
LEFT: A box of Don Lino with selected cigars from the Colorado, Havana Reserve and Oro series.

DON RAMOS

A range of superior-quality, medium- to full-bodied, handmade cigars that is as popular in the UK as it is in the USA. They are made with Honduran fillers, binders and wrappers, creating a spicy flavour.

NAME	SIZE	RING GAUGE
Gigante	17cm/6¾in	47
No. 11	17cm/6¾in	47
No. 13	14.3cm/5⅝in	46
No. 14	14cm/5½in	42
Corona	14cm/5½in	42
Petit Corona	12.7cm/5in	42
No. 16	12.7cm/5in	42
No. 19	11.4cm/4½in	50
No. 20	11.4cm/4½in	42
Très Petit Corona	10.2cm/4in	42
No. 17	10.2cm/4in	42
CEDAR-LINED TUBES		
Churchill	17cm/6¾in	47
Tube No. 1	14cm/5½in	42
Tube No. 2	12.7cm/5in	42
Tube No. 3	11.4cm/4½in	42
Epicure	11.4cm/4½in	50

FROM LEFT TO RIGHT: No. 1 and tube, Petit Corona.

LEFT: The Don Ramos brand is widely available outside the USA.

DON TOMAS

This large range of superior-quality, full- to medium-bodied handmade cigars is available in three different series. The Special Edition series is made with Honduran tobacco grown from Connecticut, Dominican and Cuban seeds. The International series is made with a blend of Cuban-seed tobaccos

NAME	SIZE	RING GAUGE
STANDARD SERIES		
Gigante	21.6cm/8½in	52
Presidente	19cm/7½in	50
Panetela Larga	17.8cm/7in	38
Rothschild	11.4cm/4½in	50
SPECIAL EDITION SERIES		
No. 100	19cm/7½in	50
No. 200	16.5cm/6½in	44
No. 300	12.7cm/5in	50
No. 400	17.8cm/7in	36
No. 500	14cm/5½in	46
INTERNATIONAL SERIES		
No. 1	16.5cm/6½in	44
No. 2	14cm/5½in	50

FROM TOP TO BOTTOM: 400, 500, 300.

EL REY DEL MUNDO

El Rey del Mundo, translated as "King of the World", is an extensive range of superior-quality, full- to medium-bodied, handmade cigars produced in Honduras for J.R. Tobacco. They are not to be confused with the cigars of the same name made in Cuba – their flavour is stronger than this brand. The Honduran examples are made with an Ecuadorean Sumatran-seed wrapper and local filler and binder tobaccos. A lighter-flavoured series is made with a Connecticut Shade leaf wrapper, Dominican filler and locally grown binder tobacco. The current range has been available since 1994, and there are plans to include up to 47 different sizes.

NAME	SIZE	RING GAUGE
Coronation	21.6cm/8½in	52
Principale	20.3cm/8in	47
Robusto Supreme	18.4cm/7¼in	54
Corona Immensa	18.4cm/7¼in	47
Double Corona	17.8cm/7in	49
Flor de la Vonda	16.5cm/6½in	52
Choix Supreme	15.5cm/6⅛in	49
Robusto Larga	15.2cm/6in	54
Corona	14.3cm/5⅝in	45
Habana Club	14cm/5½in	42
Robusto	12.7cm/5in	54
Rothschild	12.7cm/5in	50
LIGHTS SERIES		
Plantation	16.5cm/6½in	30
Elegante	14.3cm/5⅝in	29
Tino	14cm/5½in	38
Reynita	12.7cm/5in	38
Très Petit Corona	12cm/4¾in	43
Petit Lonsdale	11.7cm/4⅝in	43
Café au Lait	11.4cm/4½in	35

FROM LEFT TO RIGHT: *Café au Lait, Robusto, Reynita, Tino, Elegante.*

FROM LEFT TO RIGHT: *Flor del Mundo, Corona Immensa,*
Choix Supreme, Del Mundo Tino, Petit Lonsdale.

EXCALIBUR

This range of superior-quality, full- to medium-bodied cigars is sold in the USA as the Hoyo de Monterrey Excalibur brand. Elsewhere they only bear the Excalibur label. Some people consider them to be among the best hand-made cigars available outside Cuba.

NAME	SIZE	RING GAUGE
No. I	18.4cm/7¼in	54
No. II	17cm/6¾in	47
No. III	15.5cm/6⅛in	48
No. IV	14.3cm/5⅝in	46
No. V	15.9cm/6¼in	45
No. VI	14cm/5½in	38
No. VII	12.7cm/5in	43

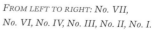

FROM LEFT TO RIGHT: No. VII,
No. VI, No. IV, No. III, No. II, No. I.

FELIPE GREGORIO

This small range of extremely good-quality, medium-flavoured, handmade, *puro* cigars was successfully introduced to the American market in 1990. The cigars are made from 100% Honduran tobacco, producing a smooth flavour.

NAME	SIZE	RING GAUGE
Glorioso	19.7cm/7¾in	50
Suntuoso	17.8cm/7in	48
Robusto	12.7cm/5in	52
Belicoso	15.2cm/6in	52
Sereno	14.6cm/5¾in	42
Nino	10.8cm/4¼in	44

FROM LEFT TO RIGHT: Belicoso, Glorioso, Suntuoso, Sereno, Robusto, Nino.

HABANA GOLD

Habana Gold comprises three different ranges of superior-quality, medium- to mild-flavoured, handmade cigars. All are made with a Nicaraguan binder and filler. The Sterling Vintage series has vintage Ecuadorean wrappers, the White Label series has a Nicaraguan wrapper and the Black Label series has an Indonesian wrapper.

NAME	SIZE	RING GAUGE
Presidente	21.6cm/8½in	52
Double Corona	19cm/7½in	46
Churchill	17.8cm/7in	52
No. 2	15.5cm/6⅛in	52
Corona	15.2cm/6in	44
Robusto	12.7cm/5in	50
Torpedo	15.2cm/6in	52
Petit Corona	12.7cm/5in	42

FROM LEFT TO RIGHT: Robusto, Torpedo, Churchill, Petit Corona.

BELOW: Habana Gold cigars are individually wrapped in cellophane within their cedar box.

HOYO DE MONTERREY

Hoyo de Monterrey cigars, made in Honduras, are some of the finest in the world. They differ from the famous Cuban brand of the same name in having a stronger, fuller flavour, particularly in the larger sizes. The range is extensive and of excellent quality. The cigars are full-bodied to medium in flavour, and are made with a filler blended from Honduran, Nicaraguan and Cuban-seed Dominican tobaccos, a Connecticut binder and a wrapper made from Sumatran-seed, Ecuadorean tobacco. The standard range should not be confused with the Excalibur series, which is very different in flavour.

NAME	SIZE	RING GAUGE
Presidente	21.6cm/8½in	52
Sultan	18.4cm/7¼in	54
Cuban Largo	18.4cm/7¼in	47
Cetro	17.8cm/7in	43
Double Corona	17cm/6¾in	48
No. 1	16.5cm/6½in	43
Churchill	15.9cm/6¼in	45
Ambassador	16cm/6¼in	44
Governor	15.5cm/6⅛in	50
Delight	15.9cm/6¼in	37
Culebra	15.2cm/6in	35
Corona	13.6cm/5⅜in	46
Café Royal	13.6cm/5⅜in	43
Dreams	14.6cm/5¾in	46
Super Hoyo	14cm/5½in	44
No. 5	13.3cm/5¼in	43
Sabroso	12.7cm/5in	40
Rothschild	11.4cm/4½in	50

FROM LEFT TO RIGHT: Governor, Ambassador. The Governor is characterized by a rich coffee flavour with chocolate overtones, making it perfect as an after-dinner smoke.

J. R. ULTIMATE

J.R. Tobacco of America is the largest mail-order, retail and wholesale purveyor of cigars in the USA. Founded by Jack Rothman and now run by his son, Lew, the company manufactures superior-quality, handmade cigars in Honduras and the Dominican Republic. Two ranges are handmade in the Dominican Republic: Special Jamaicans with Connecticut leaf wrappers, and Special Coronas with Ecuadorean wrapper and binder, and a filler with a mix of Brazilian, Honduran and Dominican tobacco. The Honduran range of superior-quality, full-bodied to medium-flavoured, handmade cigars are made with blended, locally grown Cuban-seed tobaccos for filler and binder, and a Nicaraguan wrapper.

NAME	SIZE	RING GAUGE
ULTIMATE SERIES		
Estelo	21.6cm/8½in	52
Presidente	21.6cm/8½in	52
Super Cetro	20.9cm/8¼in	43
Cetro	17.8cm/7in	42
Slim	17.5cm/6⅞in	36
Palma Extra	17.5cm/6⅞in	38
Double Corona	17cm/6¾in	48
Padron	15.2cm/6in	54
Corona	14.3cm/5⅝in	45
Small Cetro	14cm/5½in	38
Small Corona	11.7cm/4⅝in	43
Rothschild	11.4cm/4½in	50
No. 1	18.4cm/7¼in	54
No. 5	15.5cm/6⅛in	44
No. 10	20.9cm/8¼in	47

LEFT: Palma Extra, Slim.

*FROM LEFT TO RIGHT: Cetro, No. 1,
No. 10, Super Cetro, Presidente.*

LEMPIRA

This range is made in Honduras by Tropical Tobacco Inc. using a blended filler from Honduras and Nicaragua. The binder is grown in the Dominican Republic from Havana seed and the wrapper is a Connecticut Shade leaf. This is a medium-strength cigar with an abundance of flavour.

NAME	SIZE	RING GAUGE
Presidente	19.7cm/7¾in	50
Lancero	19cm/7½in	38
Churchill	17.8cm/7in	48
Lonsdale	16.5cm/6½in	44
Toro	15.2cm/6in	50
Corona	14cm/5½in	42
Robusto	12.7cm/5in	50

FROM LEFT TO RIGHT: Robusto, Lonsdale, Presidente.

PADRON

This range of good-quality, medium- to mild-flavoured, handmade cigars is made with 100% Nicaraguan tobacco in Nicaragua and Honduras. The brand was originally founded in Miami, Florida, in the 1960s.

NAME	SIZE	RING GAUGE
Magnum	23cm/9in	50
Grand Reserve	20.3cm/8in	41
Churchill	17.5cm/6⁷⁄₈in	46
Panetela	17.5cm/6⁷⁄₈in	36
Palma	16cm/6⁵⁄₁₆in	42
Londre	14cm/5½in	42
Delicia	12.4cm/4⁷⁄₈in	46
No. 2000	12.7cm/5in	50
No. 3000	14cm/5½in	52
1964 ANNIVERSARY SERIES		
Diplomatico	17.8cm/7in	50
Monarca	16.5cm/6½in	46
Superior	16.5cm/6½in	42
Corona	15.2cm/6in	42
Exclusivo	14cm/5½in	50

BELOW: No. 2000

PARTICULARES

This small range of cigars is made in Honduras by Tropical Tobacco Inc. using Honduran filler. The binder is Havana-seed tobacco grown in Honduras and the wrapper is from Ecuador. This is considered a mild- to medium-strength cigar.

NAME	SIZE	RING GAUGE
Viajante	21.6cm/8½in	52
Presidente	19.7cm/7¾in	50
Supremo	17.8cm/7in	43
Churchill	17.5cm/6⅞in	49
Panetela	17.5cm/6⅞in	35
Royal Corona	15.9cm/6¼in	43
Matador	15.2cm/6in	50
Petit	14.3cm/5⅝in	34
Numero Cuatro	14cm/5½in	42
Rothschild	12.7cm/5in	50

LEFT: *Rothschild*

RIGHT: *Particulares cigars are packaged in wooden boxes with sliding lids.*

PETRUS

Launched in 1990, this range of good-quality, mild, handmade cigars has proved to be very popular. The cigars are made with Connecticut-seed wrapper from Ecuador and Honduran binder and filler.

NAME	SIZE	RING GAUGE
Lord Byron	20.3cm/8in	38
Double Corona	19.7cm/7¾in	50
Churchill	17.8cm/7in	50
No. 2	15.9cm/6¼in	44
Palma Fina	15.2cm/6in	38
Corona Sublime	14cm/5½in	46
Antonius	12.7cm/5in	52
Gregorius	12.7cm/5in	42
Rothschild	12cm/4¾in	50
Duchess	11.4cm/4½in	30

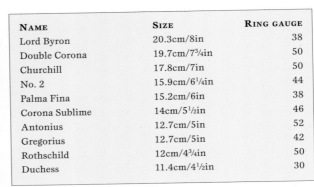

FROM LEFT TO RIGHT: Corona Sublime, Churchill, Gregorius, Antonius, Rothschild.

PUNCH

Not to be confused with the well-known Cuban cigars of the same name, the Honduran range of Punch handmade cigars is extremely well-made, with a medium to mild flavour. The cigars are made with a filler blended from Dominican, Nicaraguan and Honduran tobaccos, a Connecticut binder and Sumatran-seed Ecuadorean wrapper. The Grand Cru series is aged for at least three years.

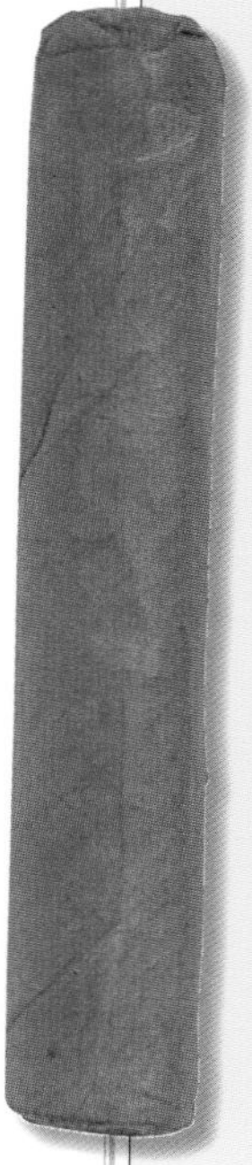

RIGHT: Rothschild

NAME	SIZE	RING GAUGE
STANDARD SERIES		
President	21.6cm/8½in	52
Diadema	18.4cm/7¼in	52
After Dinner	18.4cm/7¼in	45
Elegant	18.1cm/7⅛in	36
Casa Grande	17.8cm/7in	46
Largo Elegante	17.8cm/7in	32
Double Corona	16.8cm/6⅝in	48
Bristol	15.9cm/6¼in	50
Amatista	15.9cm/6¼in	44
Punch	15.5cm/6⅛in	43
Café Royal	14.6cm/5¾in	44
No. 75	14cm/5½in	44
Rothschild	11.4cm/4½in	48
GRAND CRU SERIES		
Prince Consort	21.6cm/8½in	52
Diadema	18.4cm/7¼in	54
Tubed Monarca	17cm/6¾in	48
SELECCION DE LUXE SERIES		
Château Lafite	18.4cm/7¼in	54
Corona	15.9cm/6¼in	45
Château Margaux	14.6cm/5¾in	46

FROM LEFT TO RIGHT: *Amatista, Café Royal, Punch, Largo Elegante, No. 75.*

FROM LEFT TO RIGHT: *Diadema,
Largo Elegante, Casa Grande,
After Dinner, President.*

JAMAICA

Jamaica is an independent island nation of the Commonwealth that lies in the West Indies, 90 miles south of Cuba. It was discovered in 1494 by Christopher Columbus and was occupied by the Spanish until the mid-17th century, when British forces successfully invaded and occupied the island. Jamaica remained a British colony until full independence in 1962. It is a mainly mountainous country with a tropical, maritime climate.

Although most people work in agriculture, the principal sources of income are provided by tourism, sugar cane and mining. During the last half of the 19th century many cigar-makers emigrated to Jamaica to escape the oppressive Spanish colonial regime in Cuba. They set up factories in Kingston, and to this day, a few brands of superior-quality, mild, handmade Jamaican cigars are still available for the cigar aficionado. Of these, the best known are the Macanudo brand and the Temple Hall brand.

BELOW: Montego Bay, Jamaica. Although the country produces only a few cigars, they are highly esteemed by the cigar aficionado.

CIFUENTES

The intertwined letters "C" and "R", which form the monogram on the lid of Cifuentes cigars, stand for Ramon Cifuentes, who created them during his tenure as cigar master of the Partagas factory in Havana in 1876. They are now made in Jamaica by General Cigar Company, using three types of Piloto Cubano filler tobaccos grown in the Dominican Republic, and a Jember binder and Connecticut Shade wrapper, grown on the company's own farms. The result is a superior cigar with a deeply mellow flavour.

NAME	SIZE	RING GAUGE
Churchill	18.4cm/7¼in	49
Fancytail	17cm/6¾in	42
Belicoso	15.9cm/6¼in	50
Toro	15.2cm/6in	49
Rothschild	12cm/4¾in	49

FROM LEFT TO RIGHT: *Churchill, Belicoso, Toro, Rothschild, Fancytail.*

BELOW: *The cigars are packed in boxes originally designed in 1876, with Don Ramon's portrait on the inside lid.*

MACANUDO

These superior-quality, handmade cigars, one of the most popular brands in the USA, were first made in Jamaica in 1868. They are now manufactured by the General Cigar Company, both in Jamaica and also in the Dominican Republic. As the same blend of tobaccos is used in both locations, it is extremely difficult to differentiate between their countries of origin. Apart from the Vintage Range, which is made only in Jamaica, Macanudo all use Connecticut wrappers, Mexican binders and Jamaican, Mexican and Dominican fillers. Only Macanudo ages the wrapper leaf a second time, just as it used to be done in Cuba.

LEFT: *Vintage No. II*   RIGHT: *Vintage No. III*

NAME	SIZE	RING GAUGE
Prince of Wales	20.3cm/8in	52
Prince Philip	19cm/7½in	49
Portofino	17.8cm/7in	34
Baron de Rothschild	16.5cm/6½in	42
Duke of Windsor	15.2cm/6in	50
Claybourne	15.2cm/6in	31
Hampton Court	14.6cm/5¾in	43
Crystal	14cm/5½in	50
Hyde Park	14cm/5½in	49
Duke of Devon	14cm/5½in	42
Petit Corona	12.7cm/5in	38
Ascot	10.6cm/4³⁄₁₆in	32
Caviar	10.2cm/4in	36
Miniature	9.5cm/3¾in	24
VINTAGE SERIES		
No. I	19cm/7½in	49
No. II	16.7cm/6⁹⁄₁₆in	43
No. III	14.1cm/5⁹⁄₁₆in	43
No. IV	11.4cm/4½in	47
No. V	14cm/5½in	49

TEMPLE HALL

Temple Hall was a tobacco plantation originally founded by Cuban émigrés in 1876, in the mountains of Jamaica. There the combination of rich soil, dependable rainfall and wind-sheltered fields produced tobacco crops of highly superior quality. The Temple Hall brand was re-introduced by the General Cigar Company in 1992. The excellent quality, mild- to medium-flavoured, handmade cigars are made with a Connecticut Shade wrapper, Mexican binders from the San Andrés Valley region and a filler blended from Dominican, Mexican and Jamaican tobaccos.

NAME	SIZE	RING GAUGE
No. 500	12.7cm/5in	31
No. 550	14cm/5½in	49
No. 625	15.9cm/6¼in	42
No. 675	17cm/6¾in	45
No. 700	17.8cm/7in	49
Belicoso	15.2cm/6in	50
No. 450 Maduro	11.4cm/4½in	49

FROM LEFT TO RIGHT: Belicoso, 675, 500, 700.

RIGHT: Temple Hall, an esteemed Jamaican brand, was re-introduced by General Cigar in recent years.

MEXICO

ong before Christopher Columbus arrived in Central America, the Mayan Indians were smoking rolled-up tobacco leaves. Tobacco growing is now one of the country's main industries and Mexico is a major producer of cigars, including premium types with a mild to heavy flavour. Probably the best known of the Mexican handmade cigars are the Matacan, Santa Clara, Te-Amo and Veracruz brands. The Matacan brand is made by the Consolidated Cigar Corporation in the San Andrés Valley. These cigars are well-made with a medium- to full-bodied flavour. The excellent mild- to medium-flavoured Santa

Clara brand was founded in 1830 and is made from 100% Mexican tobacco. Also made by the Consolidated Cigar Company is the Te-Amo range of handmade cigars. Te-Amo are made in the San Andrés Valley in a large range of sizes. Finally, the Veracruz range of superior handmade cigars, also made in the San Andrés Valley, was founded in 1977 by Oscar Franck Terrazas and is sold mainly in the USA. The larger sizes of this brand are packaged in glass tubes and then packed in individual cedar boxes to ensure the cigars' freshness.

BELOW: Mexico produces a small range of highly regarded hand-rolled cigars.

TE-AMO

This range of good-quality, mild to medium, handmade cigars is produced by the Consolidated Cigar Corporation in the tobacco-growing area of the San Andrés valley. Te-Amo (Spanish for "I love you") cigars are very popular in the USA. The range is made from 100% Mexican tobacco.

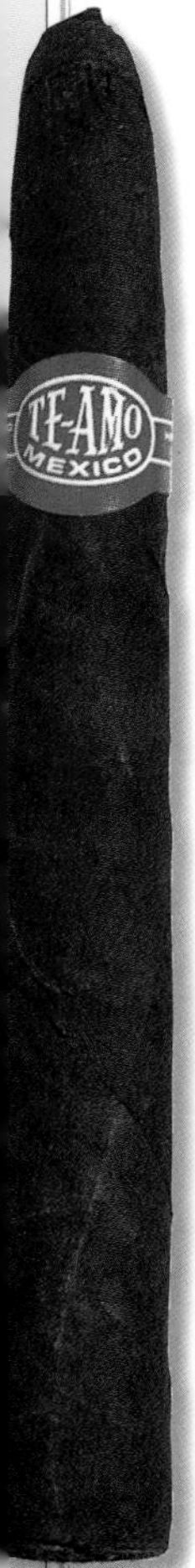

NAME	SIZE	RING GAUGE
CEO	21.6cm/8½in	52
Gran Piramide	19.7cm/7¾in	54
Presidente	17.8cm/7in	50
Relaxation	16.8cm/6⅝in	44
Toro	15.2cm/6in	50
Satisfaction	15.2cm/6in	46
Meditation	15.2cm/6in	42
Elegante	14.6cm/5¾in	27
Torito	12cm/4¾in	50

FROM LEFT TO RIGHT: Gran Piramide, Torito, Meditation, Satisfaction, Toro Maduro, Presidente.

VERACRUZ

A range of excellent-quality, mild to medium, handmade cigars produced in the tobacco-growing area of the San Andrés Valley in the state of Veracruz. The brand was founded in the 1970s and is popular in the USA. A great feature of the larger sizes is the packaging. The cigars are sealed in glass tubes with a foam and rubber stopper, and then wrapped in tissue paper before being packed in individual cedar boxes. This ensures that the cigars are fresh, but adds significantly to the cost.

NAME	SIZE	RING GAUGE
Veracruz Magnum	20cm/7⅞in	48
Mina de Veracruz	15.9cm/6¼in	42
Veracruz l'Operetta	12.4cm/4⅞in	34
Poema de Veracruz	15.9cm/6¼in	42
Flor de Veracruz	11.7cm/4⅝in	34

FROM LEFT TO RIGHT: Veracruz Magnum, Poema de Veracruz, Veracruz l'Operetta.

NICARAGUA

Nicaragua is the largest republic in Central America, lying between Honduras and Costa Rica. It has a damp, tropical climate, and about half of the land is under forestation. Most of the sparse population works in agriculture, which includes the growing of tobacco. Discovered in 1502 by Christopher Columbus, the country had a mixture of British and Spanish rulers, and later became part of the Mexican empire. It achieved full independence in 1838. Following a short, self-imposed presidency by an American, William Walker, there followed many years of peace until 1912, when civil war broke out. The country was then occupied by US forces until 1933. From 1937 until the late 1970s, Nicaragua was ruled by the father-and-son presidency of the Somoza family. This was followed by the harsh Sandanista regime and a bloody civil war.

ABOVE: Cutting tobacco on Piedra Azul state farm.

BELOW: Tobacco pickers waiting to be paid. Most of the population of Nicaragua works in agriculture.

Before the civil war, Nicaraguan cigars were considered to be the next best smoke to a Havana. However, the industry suffered terribly in the fighting, with most of the tobacco plantations and barns being destroyed. Since the early 1990s, efforts have been made to re-establish the cigar industry. In particular, the good-quality Joya de Nicaragua brand has shown much improvement, with the maturation of the better local tobaccos used in its manufacture. Other brands of handmade cigars made in Nicaragua include Habanica and Padron. Nicaraguan cigars are full-bodied and aromatic, with a mild to medium taste.

JOYA DE NICARAGUA

This range of excellent-quality, medium-bodied, handmade cigars has re-established itself in the marketplace following the disruption caused by the civil war in Nicaragua. They are made with a Connecticut Shade wrapper and locally grown tobacco is used for both filler and binder.

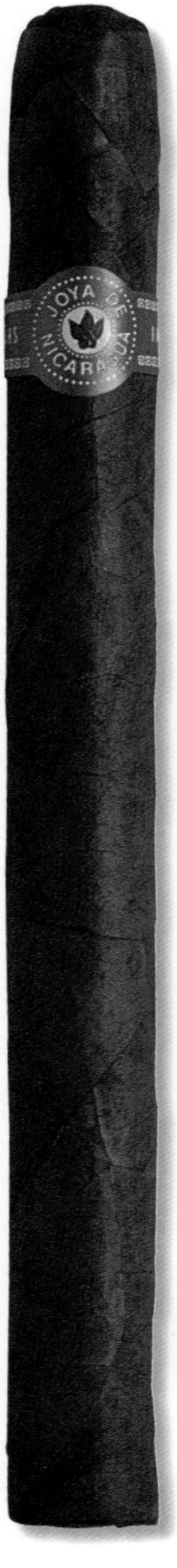

NAME	SIZE	RING GAUGE
Viajante	21.6cm/8½in	52
Churchill	17.5cm/6⅞in	49
No. 1	16.8cm/6⅝in	44
No. 5	17.5cm/6⅞in	35
No. 10	16.5cm/6½in	43
Elegante	16.5cm/6½in	38
No. 6	15.2cm/6in	52
Corona	14.3cm/5⅝in	48
Petit	14cm/5½in	38
Senorita	14cm/5½in	34
Petit Corona	12.7cm/5in	42
Consul	11.4cm/4½in	52
No. 2	11.4cm/4½in	41
Piccolino	10.5cm/4⅛in	30
MADURO DE LUXE		
Presidente	19cm/7½in	54
Toro	15.2cm/6in	50
Robusto	12cm/4¾in	52

FROM LEFT TO RIGHT: Viajante, Petit.

BELOW: No 2

PADRON

This range of good quality, medium- to mild-flavoured, handmade cigars is made with 100% Nicaraguan tobacco in Nicaragua and Honduras. The brand was originally founded in Miami, Florida, in the 1960s. The Anniversary series was introduced in 1994 to commemorate three decades of cigar success.

NAME	SIZE	RING GAUGE
Magnum	23cm/9in	50
Grand Reserve	20.3cm/8in	41
Executive	19cm/7½in	50
Churchill	17.5cm/6⅞in	46
Ambassador	17.5cm/6⅞in	42
Panetela	17.5cm/6⅞in	36
Palma	16cm/6⁵⁄₁₆in	42
No. 3000	14cm/5½in	52
Londres	14cm/5½in	42
Chico	14cm/5½in	36
No. 2000	12.7cm/5in	50
Delicia	12.4cm/4⅞in	46
1964 ANNIVERSARY SERIES		
Diplomatico	17.8cm/7in	50
Monarca	16.5cm/6½in	46
Superior	16.5cm/6½in	42
Corona	15.2cm/6in	42
Exclusivo	14cm/5½in	50

FROM LEFT TO RIGHT: *Delicia, Londres, Chico, Palma, Ambassador.*

THE PHILIPPINES

In the 17th century a Spanish galleon brought 200 ounces of Cuban tobacco seeds to the Philippines, then a Spanish colony. The seeds were distributed among religious missionaries, who found in the Rio Grande de Cagayan the perfect location for growing tobacco. The tobacco industry flourished in the tropical climate, and 50 years later, a gift of two cases of hand-rolled cigars was presented to the Viceroy of New Spain, as the colony was then known. In 1881, cigar companies in Manila united to establish the largest cigar factory in the Philippines. It was named La Flor de la Isabela, "The Flower of Isabela", after the tobacco cultivated in Isabela, Cagayan. The company continues to manufacture fine hand-made cigars to this day.

BELOW: The tropical climate of the Philippines is ideal for growing tobacco. Brands, such as Double Happiness, are highly regarded by connoisseurs.

DOUBLE HAPPINESS

Double Happiness cigars are produced by the curiously named Splendid Seed Company. They are handmade using prime Filipino binder and filler, which are grown in the lower Cagayan Valley, combined with a double-fermented Brazilian Sumatra wrapper.

NAME	SIZE	RING GAUGE
Ecstasy	17.8cm/7in	47
Nirvana	15.2cm/6in	52
Euphoria	16.5cm/6½in	50
Bliss	13cm/5⅛in	48
Rapture	12.7cm/5in	50

FROM TOP TO BOTTOM: Rapture, Bliss, Ecstasy.

LA FLOR DE LA ISABELA

La Flor de la Isabela was formed in 1881, when several cigar factories in Manila united to become the Philippines' largest cigar factory. Since then, the company has manufactured handmade cigars, such as the 1881 and the Tabacalera series, and also produces machine-made cigars.

THE UNITED STATES

Tobacco has been grown in the USA since the scattered tribes from the Mayan civilization travelled to North America. With them they took the tobacco plant, which was subsequently cultivated by native Americans for both medicinal and religious purposes. The first European settlers founded communities in Virginia in 1608, and by 1612 had set up the first tobacco plantations. The locally

BELOW: Some of the best wrappers in the world are grown in the United States.

grown tobacco was smoked in pipes, until the first consignment of Cuban cigars in the 18th century.

In the early 1760s, Israel Putnam returned home to Connecticut from Cuba, with a selection of Havana cigars and large amounts of Cuban tobacco seed. Connecticut had been a tobacco-growing area since the 17th century, and by the early 19th century, cigar factories had opened around Hartford, using leaves from the plants grown from the imported Cuban seed. At the same time Cuban cigars started to be imported into North America in significant quantities. Nowadays, tobacco grown in Connecticut supplies some of the best wrapper leaves in the world, outside Cuba.

The sandy loam of the Connecticut Valley in New England is ideal for growing premium-quality tobacco. The best wrappers are grown under huge tents and are known as Connecticut Shade. They are expensive to produce and can add as much as $1 (£1.60) to the price of a cigar. Drying and maturing the leaves is the same as in Cuba, except that gas burners give additional heat. They are used in the very best cigars, such as Dominican Davidoffs and Jamaican Macanudos.

By the time of the American Civil War (1861–5), cigar smoking had become widespread throughout the country. Following tax reductions in the 1870s, cigars became more readily available and domestic production increased. By the end of the 19th century, as in Europe, the cigar had become a major status

ABOVE: *Miami, Florida, is the site for the manufacture of La Gloria Cubana, one of the best-known brands of handmade cigars in the USA.*

symbol. To combat the growing popularity of cigarettes, machine production was introduced in the 1920s and this reduced the quantity of handmade cigars produced considerably.

During the last quarter of the 19th century, many Cuban cigar-makers fled from Spanish-controlled Cuba to Tampa and Key West in Florida. Nowadays, most cigars made in the USA are machine-made, such as the Cuesta-Rey series, which is still made in Tampa, and is an excellent example of its kind. Cuesta-Rey was one of the greatest cigar houses of Tampa, founded in 1884. However, Cuesta-Rey hand-made cigars are all now made in the Dominican Republic. Other well-known, machine-made brands include Arango, Directors, Garcia y Vega, Havana Blend (using 100% Cuban tobacco) and King Edward. The best-known handmade brand still made in the USA is the superb La Gloria Cubana range, manufactured in Miami using Ecuadorean wrappers, and fillers and binders from Nicaragua, Ecuador or the Dominican Republic.

The overall cigar market in the USA has experienced rapid growth since 1993, reversing a steady decline in the market from 1964. Led by a growth in mass-market, large and premium cigars, the cigar market has increased at a compound annual rate of 9.8% in unit terms between 1993–6, and has increased at almost twice that rate in retail dollar sales.

CONSOLIDATED CIGAR CORPORATION

Consolidated Cigar Corporation is the leading cigar company in the USA, selling nearly 1 billion cigars a year and commanding 25% of the market. Consolidated Cigar Corporation was formed in 1918 by Julius Lichtenstein, President of the American Sumatra Tobacco Company, leaf specialists, which amalgamated six independent cigar manufacturers. One of the six, G. H. Johnson Cigar Company, had a cigar brand called Dutch Masters. It was decided to make this brand the flagship of the new company, and over the years Dutch Masters has developed into one of the biggest brands in the USA. In 1926, Consolidated added another major brand when it purchased the G.H.P. Cigar Company. G.H.P.'s El Producto brand was promoted by the late actor and comedian George Burns, one of the best-known showbusiness smokers of all time. Julius Lichtenstein was succeeded by Alfred Silberman in 1945 and in 1948 by his son, Samuel "Buddy" Silberman, whose name was to become legendary in the cigar world.

In late 1968 Consolidated was taken over by the Gulf & Western conglomerate. The company then entered the premium, handmade cigar business, through the formation of Cuban Cigar Brands in the Canary Islands with Pepe Garcia, a major Cuban manufacturer, whose factory in Cuba had been nationalized by the Castro regime. It then acquired the Moro Cigar Company and its Primo del Rey trademark.

Gulf & Western sold Consolidated in 1983 to five of its senior managers, and 16 months later the company was sold again to MacAndrews & Forbes, a holding company controlled by Mr Ronald Perelman, chairman of Revlon, Inc. In 1986 it acquired the assets of the American Cigar Company, including Antonio y

LEFT: *Don Diego Lonsdale,* ABOVE RIGHT: *Don Diego Corona*

Cleopatra, La Corona and Roi-Tan cigars. It also purchased the Milton Sherman Tobacco Company and the pipe tobacco brands of Iwan Ries & Company.

In 1988 the President and management purchased Consolidated from MacAndrews & Forbes and immediately made three more acquisitions, Te-Amo cigars, Royal Jamaica Cigars and Century Tobacco Company's pipe tobacco products.

In 1993 the company was re-purchased by MAFCO Holdings Inc., Mr Perelman's personal company, and later in 1996 it went public.

Today the company employs about 5,000 people and has its headquarters in Fort Lauderdale. It operates production facilities in Honduras, Puerto Rico, Pennsylvania, Jamaica, Virginia and the Dominican Republic, as well as Mexico, Brazil and Holland. Leaf supplies are obtained from growers in every part of the globe. The company's trademarks include Antonio y Cleopatra, Don Diego, Dutch Masters, Dutch Treats, El Producto, Flamenco, Henry Clay, H. Upmann, La Corona, Mixture 79, Montecristo, Montecruz, Muriel, Primo del Rey, Roi-Tan, Royal Jamaica, Santa Damiana, Te-Amo and Three Star.

ABOVE FROM LEFT TO RIGHT:
Antonio y Cleopatra Tubos and tube.

FROM LEFT TO RIGHT: Antonio y Cleopatra Grenadier,
Antonio y Cleopatra Paloma Maduro.

THE ORIGINAL KEY WEST CIGAR FACTORY

In 1965, Eleanor Walsh established the Original Key West Cigar Factory. When it was founded there were a few cigar factories remaining in Key West from the turn of the century. These other factories eventually closed, while the Original Key West Cigar Factory thrived. For the first 25 years the factory employed three people: the owner and two rollers. With each sale, Eleanor distributed a price list and a book of matches and from there the business grew by word of mouth. The company has now expanded through mail order and has many loyal customers. Original customers come back to Key West to visit the factory, and visitors can still see the room where the first cigars were purchased from the Original Key West Cigar Factory.

The company has retained many of the traditional skills associated with handmade cigars, and on any day visitors may view the cigar rollers demonstrating the difficult art of hand-rolling a fine cigar. Three ranges of cigars are made. The long filler cigars are hand-rolled with Cuban-seed Honduran tobacco and an Ecuadorean wrapper, and

LEFT TO RIGHT: Figuardo Torpedo, Jamaican Rhum, House Special.

come in 13 varieties. This combination of tobaccos presents a very mild and smooth cigar. The premium-aged long filler cigars are hand-rolled with an aged Cuban-seed Honduran tobacco, a Cameroon wrapper and come in seven sizes. These cigars are full-bodied and spicy yet mild. The blended cigars are hand-rolled with a blend of various Cuban-seed Honduran tobaccos and come in four sizes. Included in the mild blends are the Rhum cigars which have a slight sweetness and a very aromatic flavour.

LEFT TO RIGHT: Harry Truman, Cayo Hueso Panetela, El Hemingway.

NAME	SIZE	RING GAUGE
LONG FILLER CIGARS		
Key West Caballero	20.3cm/8in	39
El Presidente	20cm/7⅞in	50
Key West Diplomat	17.8cm/7in	48
Cayo Hueso Panetela	17.8cm/7in	36
Carmencita	17.8cm/7in	
Super Fino	17.8cm/7in	
Churchill	17.8cm/7in	50
Elegante	15.2cm/6in	50
Coronado	15.2cm/6in	48
El Hemingway	13.3cm/5¼in	46
House Special	12.7cm/5in	50
Cuban Split	12.7cm/5in	36
Small Conchita	10.2cm/4in	
PREMIUM-AGED LONG FILLER CIGARS		
Harry Truman	17.8cm/7in	48
Conchita Panetela	17.8cm/7in	36
Figuardo Torpedo	15.2cm/6in	56
Gran Corona	15.2cm/6in	48
Mini-Robusto	12.7cm/5in	46
BLENDED CIGARS		
Pirates Alley Panetela	17.8cm/7in	38
Key West Queen	13.3cm/5¼in	50
Jamaican Rhum	12.7cm/5in	44

MASS-MARKET
MACHINE-MADE CIGARS

For the aficionado, nothing compares to the quality of a premium hand-rolled cigar, no matter what its country of origin. For the beginner, some mass-market products merit investigation. In the United States, there has long been a tradition of good-quality affordable cigars, while in Europe, consumption of machine-made cigars is enormous.

The EU is not only a major consumer of cigars, but also a major manufacturer of machine-made ones. Among the leading cigar-manufacturing countries are the Netherlands, Spain, Germany, Denmark and Switzerland. During 1996, total cigar and cigar-illo consumption in the EU totalled 6.4 billion pieces. The leading consumer was France (1.5 billion) followed by Germany and the United Kingdom.

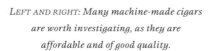

LEFT AND RIGHT: *Many machine-made cigars are worth investigating, as they are affordable and of good quality.*

THE OFFICIAL E.E.C. DEFINITION OF A CIGAR

Any tobacco product, which can be smoked as it is and which is:
♦ A roll of tobacco with an outer wrapper of natural tobacco; or
♦ A roll of tobacco containing predominantly broken or threshed leaf, with a binder of reconstituted tobacco, and with an outer wrapper which is of reconstituted tobacco, having the normal colour of a cigar and which is fitted spirally; or
♦ A roll of tobacco containing predominantly broken or threshed leaf, with an outer wrapper of reconstituted tobacco, having the normal colour of a cigar; and having a weight, exclusive of any detachable filter or mouthpiece, of not less than 2.3g (0.09oz); and having a circumference over at least one-third of its length, of not less than 34mm ($^{15}/_{16}$in).

BELGIUM

TABACOFINA-VANDER ELST

In 1874 Henri Vander Elst, a farmer's son from Wilsele, opened a specialist tobacco shop. Soon, with the help of his two brothers, François and Alphonse, he widened the scope of his business to encompass the manufacture of different tobacco products: cigars, chewing tobacco, snuff and pipe tobacco. From then on, the company, Vander Elst Frères, expanded and its success enabled factories to be built in and outside Belgium. The Turnhout factory, which was founded in 1945, specializes in cigar production and the Corps Diplomatique brand in particular. This range, with a subtle and mild taste, comes in 12 different sizes. The filler is a blend of tobacco from Java, Brazil, Havana and Sumatra and the wrappers are provided by fine Sumatran leaves.

The Mercator brand of cigars was also created by Vander Elst in 1960 and named after the famous Belgian geographer, Gerhardus Mercator, 1512–94. Mercator is known for his world maps, made for navigation purposes, but his reputation was established by the invention of geographical projections in order to obtain parallel meridians, first used in his map of 1568. The Mercator range of cigars is very wide, from the miniatures to the more traditionally shaped cigars.

FROM LEFT TO RIGHT: *Jupiter, Fiesta, Fiesta Natural, Fiesta Mild, Jupiter Mild.*

GERMANY

DANNEMANN

Dannemann is a well-known maker of small cigars. The company was founded in Brazil by Geraldo Dannemann in 1873. The cigars are machine-made in Germany, using tobacco imported from Brazil and Sumatra. The brand is now owned by the company Ritmeester Cigars of the Netherlands.

Name	Size	Ring gauge
Vera Cruz Aromatico	16.7cm/6⁹⁄₁₆in	32
Vera Cruz Ligero	16.7cm/6⁹⁄₁₆in	32
Lights Brazil	15.4cm/6¹⁄₁₆in	30
Lights Sumatra	15.4cm/6¹⁄₁₆in	30
Lonja Brazil	13.6cm/5³⁄₈in	20
Lonja Sumatra	13.6cm/5³⁄₈in	20
Espada Brazil	13.2cm/5³⁄₁₆in	44
Espada Sumatra	13.2cm/5³⁄₁₆in	44
Imperial Brazil	10.2cm/4in	20
Imperial Sumatra	10.2cm/4in	20
Moods	7.3cm/2⁷⁄₈in	20
Speciale Brazil	7cm/2³⁄₄in	22
Speciale Sumatra	7cm/2³⁄₄in	22

FROM LEFT TO RIGHT: *Lights, Imperial Brazil, Lonja and box.*

HOLLAND

The cigar has been a favourite form of smoking in the Netherlands since manufacture started at the end of the 18th century. Due to the dominance of the East Indies by the Dutch, from the beginning of the 17th century to 1945, Dutch cigars have included leaf grown firstly in Java and then Sumatra. Many Dutch cigars of today are composed of about 70% Indonesian leaf, combined with a large proportion of Brazilian and Cuban tobacco leaves. Holland is world-famous for its quality, machine-made brands of the "dry" Dutch type of cigars. All the cigars are now machine-made, some using homogenized tobacco, but many are made with the finest, aged tobaccos from Colombia, the Dominican Republic, Mexico, Java and Cameroon.

The Dutch Cigar Manufacturers Association is formed by six well-known Dutch manufacturers of cigars and cigarillos. Together, these six

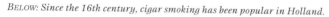

BELOW: Since the 16th century, cigar smoking has been popular in Holland.

manufacturers share over 90 % of the Dutch market and almost 100 % of the Dutch exports of cigars and cigarillos. The members of the Association and their most important brands are: Agio Sigarenfabrieken N.V. with the brands Agio, Panter, Balmoral and De Huifkar; Cadena Claassen Sigarenfabrieken B.V. with the brands Cadena Claassen, Carl Upmann and Acht Zaligheden; Swedish Match Cigars B.V. with the brands La Paz, Willem II, Karel I, Justus van Maurik and Heeren van Ruydael; Henri Wintermans Sigarenfabrieken B.V. with the brands Henri Wintermans and Café Crème; Chambord with brands Ritmeester B.V., Ritmeester, Oud Kampen, Hajenius and Danneman; and Schimmelpenninck Sigarenfabrieken B.V. which markets the one brand, Schimmelpenninck.

The Dutch cigar industry produced 1.8 billion cigars, señoritas and cigarillos in 1996, making it the second largest cigar manufacturer in the world. Of this figure, over 1.5 billion were exported to over 100 countries. The major markets for Dutch cigar export are within the European Union and they account for about 85 % of the total exports. The leading export destinations in order of importance are: France, the United Kingdom, Germany and Belgium.

During 1996 Holland imported over 21 million cigars and cigarillos from the Canary Islands and nearly 7 million from the Dominican Republic. In total the country imported 50 million cigars and cigarillos.

AGIO

The Agio brand of small cigars is very popular in Europe and is made with tobaccos from the Cameroon, Java and Sumatra. Its popular Mehari family of cigars comes in three different types: Mild & Light (light Connecticut wrappers with a light touch of Burley), Brasil (dark Brazilian wrapper leaves with a full-flavoured filler mixture) and Cameroon (with Cameroon wrappers).

NAME	SIZE	RING GAUGE
Mehari's Sumatra	10.2cm/4in	23
Mehari's Mild	10.2cm/4in	23
Senoritas Red Label	10.2cm/4in	21
Biddies Brasil	8.3cm/3¼in	20
Filter Tipped	7.6cm/3in	21

HENRI WINTERMANS

In December 1996, the Scandinavian Tobacco Group of Companies (ST), Copenhagen, acquired Henri Wintermans Sigarenfabrieken B.V. from the British-American Tobacco Company. This merger created the largest cigar manufacturer in Europe, with a combined annual output in the region of one billion cigars. The new company, which retains the internationally-renowned name of Henri Wintermans, is one of the leading cigar exporters in the world, with a global distribution network spanning over 100 countries. The headquarters of Henri Wintermans is in Eersel, Holland, and the company employs almost 2,000 people in factories, warehouses and tobacco-processing plants, stretching from the Dominican Republic through Europe.

The new Henri Wintermans range, which includes Small Cigars, Half Coronas and Coronas de Luxe, represents the best Dutch tradition of blending and cigar-making. The company also manufactures Slim Panetelas, Slim Señoritas, Excellentes and Slim Coronas. The tobaccos are

BELOW: Henri Wintermans is one of the leading cigar exporters in the world, with a highly regarded and well-known range of cigars.

Name	Size	Ring gauge
Excellente	16cm/6¼in	42
Long Panetela	13cm/5⅛in	30
Slim Panetela	13cm/5⅛in	30
Corona de Luxe	11.5cm/4½in	42
Half Corona	9.5cm/3¾in	30
Scooters	9cm/3½in	20

double-aged: the leaves are left for two years to mature and the rolled cigars are then aged for a second time, over cedarwood shelves, to create a round and full-bodied taste. The range is aimed at consumers in the medium to high end of the international cigar market, who may have graduated from mainstream brands, but who are not yet regular smokers of premium brands.

The company also produces the Café Crème range, which is the best-selling small cigar in the world. Variants include Café Crème Mild, Café Crème Rich Aroma, Café Crème Noir and Café Crème Filter Tip.

FROM LEFT TO RIGHT: *Corona de Luxe,*
Slim Panetela Cigar, Small Cigar
(part of the new Wintermans range),
Half Corona.

SCHIMMELPENNINCK

In 1924, two brothers by the name of Van Schuppen became partners in their uncle's firm, Geurts. At that time Geurts was a small cigar factory employing 21 people. This company, Geurts & Van Schuppen, started making cigars under the Schimmelpenninck brand. Schimmelpenninck is the name of a famous Dutchman, who was governor of Holland in the early 19th century. The factory was just one of the many local family companies which existed at that time, manufacturing handmade cigars to its own specifications. Until 1930 it showed very little expansion.

In 1931, the Van Schuppen brothers started a policy of mechanization, and this, together with more attractive packaging and improved sales methods, resulted in a growth to one of the larger factories in Holland. After World War II the company linked with the firm of Carreras in 1963 and was then bought by Rothmans in 1972. Since that time exports of Schimmelpenninck cigars have increased strongly and the brand is sold in more than 130 countries around the world.

ABOVE: Schimmelpenninck cigars are attractively packaged and sold worldwide.

Name	Size	Ring gauge
Duet Brazil	14.3cm/5⁵⁄₈in	27
Vada	9.8cm/3⁷⁄₈in	30
Florina	9.8cm/3⁷⁄₈in	26
Mono	8.6cm/3³⁄₈in	27
Media	7.6cm/3in	26
Havana Mild	7.6cm/3in	26
Nostra	7.3cm/2⁷⁄₈in	27

FROM LEFT TO RIGHT: Half Corona, Havana Mild, Havana Sigue, Media, Mini Cigar, Mini Cigar Mild, Swing, Duet Panetela I, Grande.

SWITZERLAND

VILLIGER

Villiger is one of the most popular machine-made small cigars in the world. The company was founded in Switzerland in 1888 by Jean Villiger and has grown to be a large international business. The Villiger family descendants still oversee the production of over 400 million cigars that are made in Switzerland, Germany and Ireland. The distinctive cigars are exported to over 70 countries throughout the world. Some of the cigars use homogenized tobacco, but many of them are manufactured with fine aged tobaccos imported from Cameroon, Java, Mexico, Columbia and the Dominican Republic.

FROM TOP TO BOTTOM: *Villiger Export (round), Villiger Export (pressed).*

NAME	SIZE
Curly	17.8cm/7in
Tipped Villiger-Kiel Mild	16.5cm/6½in
Villiger Export Kings	13cm/5⅛in
Tipped Bunte	11.4cm/4½in
Villiger Export	10.2cm/4in
Villiger Premium No. 4	10.2cm/4in
Braniff No. 1	8.9cm/3½in
Braniff Cortos Filter Light	7.6cm/3in

PUERTO RICO

Puerto Rico is a self-governing island, set in the West Indies to the east of the island of Hispaniola. It was discovered by Christopher Columbus in 1493. The island was colonized by the Spanish from 1510 until 1898, when it was ceded to the USA following the Spanish-American War. It became a US territory in 1917 and a Commonwealth in 1952. In recent years, many American companies have been attracted to Puerto Rico by various tax incentives. Among them is the Consolidated Cigar Corporation, which manufactures several brands of mass-market cigars on the island.

FROM LEFT TO RIGHT: Dutch Masters Cameroon Elite, Dutch Masters Cadet, El Producto Bouquet, El Producto Panetela.

THE UNITED STATES

The Swisher International Group was founded in 1861 and is the leading manufacturer and seller of cigars in the world. The company sells mass-market large cigars, premium cigars and little cigars. Mass-market large cigars use natural leaf wrappers or reconstituted leaf wrappers. Premium cigars are slightly more expensive, and are generally made with a natural wrapper, binder and long filler. General Cigar Company produces a range of mass-market cigars as well as their handmade premium cigars. Popular brands include Garcia Vega and White Owl.

FROM LEFT TO RIGHT: *King Edward Invincible de Luxe, King Edward Imperial (produced by Swisher International), Garcia Vega, White Owl (produced by the General Cigar Corp.).*

UNITED KINGDOM

LONDON

Alfred Dunhill of London
30 Duke Street
London SW1Y 6DL
Tel: 0171 499 9566
Fax: 0171 499 6471

Alfred Dunhill of London
5 Royal Exchange
Cornhill
London EC3V 1LL
Tel: 0171 623 9977
Fax: 0171 623 9445

Benson & Hedges
13 Old Bond Street
London W1X 4QP
Tel: 0171 493 1825
Fax: 0171 491 2276

Burlington Bertie
57 Houndsditch
London EC3A 8AA
Tel: 0171 929 2242
Fax: 0171 929 2232

Davidoff of London
35 St James's Street
London SW1A 1HD
Tel: 0171 930 3079
Fax: 0171 930 5887

G. Smith & Son
74 Charing Cross Road
London WC4H 0BG
Tel: 0171 836 7422
Fax: 0171 836 7422

Harrods Cigar Room
Knightsbridge
London SW1X 7XL
Tel: 0171 730 1234

Havana Club
165 Sloane Street
London SW1X 9QF
Tel: 0171 245 0890
Fax: 0171 245 0895

J. J. Fox of St James's
19 St. James's Street
London SW1A 1ES
Tel: 0171 930 3787
Fax: 0171 495 0097

Jayems
125 Victoria Street
London SW1E 5LA
Tel: 0171 828 1472

Sautter of Mayfair
106 Mount Street
London W1Y 5HE
Tel: 0171 499 4866
Fax: 0171 499 4866

The Segar & Snuff Parlour
27a The Market
Covent Garden
London WC2
Tel: 0171 836 8345

Selfridges Cigar Department
400 Oxford Street
London W1A 1AB
Tel: 0171 629 1234
Fax: 0171 491 1880

Shervingtons
337 High Holborn
London WC1V 7PX
Tel: 0171 405 2929
Fax: 0181 803 8887

Walter Thurgood
161–162 Salisbury House
London Wall
London EC2M 5QD
Tel: 0171 628 5437
Fax: 0171 930 5887

Wards of Gresham Street
60 Gresham Street
London EC2V 7BB
Tel: 0171 606 4318
Fax: 0171 606 4318

THE SOUTH

Burkitts
117 Church Road
Hove
East Sussex BN3 2AF
Tel: 01273 731351

Coster & Son
52 High Street
Marlow
Bucks SL7 1AW
Tel: 01628 482045
Fax: 01628 488998

Dome Tobacconist
2 Dome Building
The Quadrant
Richmond
Surrey TW9 1DT
Tel: 0181 940 3001

Harrison & Simmonds of
Bedford
80 High Street
Bedford MK40 1NN
Tel: 01234 266711
Fax: 01234 266711

M. Shave (Newbury)
1 The Arcade
Newbury
Berks RG14 5AD
Tel: 01635 46148

M. Shave of Reading
4 Harris Arcade
Reading
Berks RG1 1DN
Tel: 01734 595670

WALES AND THE WEST

C. A. Wrigley
35 Baldwin Street
Bristol BS1 1RG
Tel: 01179 273676

Frederick Tranter
5 Church Street
Abbey Green
Bath BA1 1NL
Tel: 01225 466197
Fax: 01225 466197

Lewis Darbey & Co
28–32 Wyndham Arcade
Mill Lane
Cardiff CF1 1FJ
Tel: 01222 233443

McGahey the Tobacconist
245 High Street
Exeter EX4 3NZ
Tel: 01392 496111
Fax: 01392 496113

MIDLANDS AND EAST ANGLIA

Churchills of Norwich
32 St Andrews Street
Norwich
Norfolk NR2 4AF
Tel: 01603 626437

Gauntleys of Nottingham
4 High Street
Nottingham NG1 2ET
Tel: 01159 417973
Fax: 01159 509519

Harrison & Simmonds of Cambridge
17 St John's Street
Cambridge CB2 1TW
Tel: 01223 324515
Fax: 01223 324515

J. M. Edwards
24 Fountain Street
Hanley
Stoke on Trent
Staffs SD1 1LD
Tel: 01782 281416
Fax: 01782 204246

John Hollingsworth & Son Ltd
5 Temple Row
Birmingham B2 5LG
Tel: 0121 236 7768
Fax: 0121 236 3696

John Hollingsworth & Son Ltd
97 High Street
Solihull B91 3SW
Tel: 0121 705 4549
Fax: 0121 705 4549

Lands (Tobacconists) Ltd
29 Central Chambers
Henley Street
Stratford upon Avon
Warwickshire CV37 6QN
Tel: 01789 292508

Tobacco World
(Cheltenham)
Unit F7
Regent Arcade
Cheltenham
Gloucestershire GL50 1JZ
Tel: 01242 222037
Fax: 01242 222037

THE NORTH

Arthur Morris Ltd
71 Bradshawgate
Bolton BL1 1QD
Tel: 01204 521340
Fax: 01204 521340

Birchalls of Blackpool Ltd
10 Clifton Street
Blackpool FY1 1JP
Tel: 01253 24218
Fax: 01253 291659

C. Aston
23 Minden Parade
Bury BL9 0QD
Tel: 0161 764 2026

Greens Tobacconist
37 The Headrow
Leeds LS1 6PU
Tel: 0113 244 4895
Fax: 0113 245 9417

James Barber
33 Kirkgate
Otley LS21 3HN
Tel: 01943 462603
Fax: 01943 468770

Marhaba Newsagents
39 Cross Street
Manchester M2 4LE
Tel: 0161 834 9744

Tobacco World of Chester
78 Northgate Street
Chester CH1 2HT
Tel: 01244 348821
Fax: 01244 348821

SCOTLAND

Dallings of Ayr
5 Burns Statue Square
Ayr KY7 1SU
Tel: 01292 265799
Fax: 01292 265799

Herbert Love
31 Queensferry Street
Edinburgh EH2 4QU
Tel: 0131 225 8082
Fax: 0131 225 8082

House of Gowrie
90 South Street
Perth PH2 8PD
Tel: 01738 626919
Fax: 01738 626919

The Pipe Shop
92 Leith walk
Edinburgh EH6 5HB
Tel: 0131 553 3561
Fax: 0131 555 2591

Robert Graham & Co
71 St Vincent Street
Glasgow G2 5TF
Tel: 0141 221 6588
Fax: 0141 221 6588

Steve Silletts
166 King Street
Aberdeen AB24 5BD
Tel: 01224 644455

Tobacco House
9 St Vincent Place
Glasgow G1 2DW
Tel: 0141 226 4586
Fax: 0141 226 4586

UNITED STATES

NEW YORK

Alfred Dunhill Ltd
420 Park Avenue
New York, NY
Tel: 212 753 9292

Arnold's Cigar Store
323 Madison Avenue
New York, NY
Tel: 212 697 1477

Barclay-Rex Inc.
70 E. 42nd Street
New York, NY
Tel: 212 962 3355

The Big Cigar Company
193 A Grand Street
New York, NY
Tel: 212 966 9122

Cigar Emporium
541 Warren Street
New York, NY
Tel: 518 828 5014

Davidoff of Geneva
535 Madison Avenue
54th Street
New York, NY
Tel: 212 751 9060

De La Concha
Tobacconists
1390 Avenue of the
Americas
New York, NY
Tel: 212 757 3167

J.R. Tobacco
11 E.45th Street
New York, NY
Tel: 212 983 4160

Nat Sherman Inc.
500 Fifth Avenue
New York, NY
Tel: 212 246 5500

North Cigar Lounge
483 Columbus Avenue
New York, NY
Tel: 212 595 5033

The Smoking Shop
45 Christopher Street
New York, NY
Tel: 212 929 1151

OUTSIDE NEW YORK

Diebels Sportsmens
Gallery
426 Ward Parkway
Kansas City, KS
Tel: 800 305 2988

Georgetown Tobacco
3144 M North West
Washington, DC
Tel: 202 338 5100

Holt Cigar Co. Inc.
1522 Walnut Street
Philadelphia PA
Tel: 800 523 1641

The Humidor Inc.
6900 San Pedro Avenue
San Antonio TX
Tel: 210 824 1209

Jack Schwartz Importers
175 W. Jackson
Chicago, IL
Tel: 312 782 7898

J. R. Tobacco of America
Inc.
I-95 at Route 70
Selma AL
Tel: 800 572 4427

The Owl Shop
268 College Street
New Haven, CT
Tel: 203 624 3250

The Pipe Squire
346 Coddrington Center
Santa Rosa, CA
Tel: 707 573 8544

Rich Cigar Store Inc.
801 Southwest Alder St
Portland, OR
Tel: 800 669 1527

Tinder Box Santa Monica
2729 Wilshire Boulevard
Santa Monica, CA
Tel: 310 828 4511

CANADA

BRITISH COLUMBIA

Casa de Malahato
@ Malahat Chalet
265 Malahat Drive
Malahat V0R 2L0
Tel: (604) 478 0812

Sheffield & Sons
Tobacconist
320-A 4741 Lakelse Avenue
Terrace V8G 1R5
Tel: (604) 635-9661

VANCOUVER

Alpha Tobacco
927 Denman Street
Vancouver V6G 2L9
Tel: (604) 688 1555

R J Clarke Tobacconist
3 Alexander Street
Vancouver V6A 1B2
Tel: (604) 681 8021

Vancouver Cigar Company
1938 Broadway
Vancouver V6J 1Z2

TORONTO

Groucho & Company
150 Bloor St W
Toronto M5S 2XY
Tel: (416) 922 4817

Havana House
87 Avenue Road
Toronto M5R 3R9
Tel: (416) 927 9070

QUEBEC

Davidoff
1452 rue Sherbrooke W
Montreal H3G 1K4
Tel: (514) 289 9118

La Casa del Habon
1434 rue Sherbrooke W
Montreal H3G 1K4
Tel: (514) 849 0037

AUSTRALIA
ADELAIDE
Tunney's
38–40 Grote Street
Tel: (08) 8231 5720

MELBOURNE
Alexander's Cigar Divan
at Crown Towers
8 Whiteman Street
Southbank
Tel: (03) 9292 7842

Baranow's Fine Cigars
P. O. Box 29
Preston Vic 3072
Tel: (03) 9479 6579
E-mail: Cigar1 @
MSN.com
Web site: HYPERLINK
HTTP://WWW.aml.com.a
ut/Cigar1.htm
HTTP://WWW.aml.com.a
ut/Cigar1.htm

Benjamin's Fine Tobacco
Shop 10, Strand Central
250 Elizabeth Street
Tel: (03) 9669 2879
E-mail: Bentob @
Netspace.net.au

J & D of Alexander's
7A–459 Toorak Rd
Toorak 342
Tel: (61) 9827 1477

SYDNEY
Alexander's Cigar Divan
at Pierpont's
Hotel Intercontinental
117 Macquarie Street
Tel: (02) 9252 0280

Sol Levy
713 George Street
Tel: (02) 9211 5628

NEW ZEALAND
Havana House, Cigars
Limited
11–19 Customs ST. W.
Auckland
Tel: 64 9 357 0037

Imperial Tobacco
295-A The Terrace
Wellington
Tel: 64 4 801 9002

SOUTH AFRICA
Wesley's
Golden Acre Plaza
Level 7, Cape Town
Tel: 27 21 21 5090

Wesley's
The Rosebank Mall
170
Johannesburg
Tel: 27 11 6333 2510

PICTURE CREDITS

t = top, b = bottom; l = left, r = right, c = centre

Colour Images Library pp127, 136, 138; Fine Art Photographic Library p145;
Robert Francis/South American Pictures p100; Images Colour Library p40 tr;
Tania Jovanovic pp10 bl and br, 23; Susan Meiselas/Magnum p133 b;
Murray Rothmans pp40 bl, 41 br, 42 t, 48, 73, 99 b; James Nachtewey/Magnum p 133 t;
Visual Arts Library p28; Alex Webb/Magnum p139; Jon Wyand pp8 b, 11 tl and br.

INDEX

Notes

Notes

Notes

Notes

Notes